The Prison Effect

THE
PRISON
EFFECT

DISCOVER HOW YOU ARE BLOCKING YOUR OWN HAPPINESS AND BREAK FREE TO ABUNDANCE AND JOY IN LIFE!

ALENA CHAPMAN

NEW YORK

NASHVILLE • MELBOURNE • VANCOUVER

THE PRISON EFFECT

*Discover How You Are Blocking Your Own Happiness and Break
Free to Abundance and Joy in Life*

Published in New York, New York, by Morgan James Publishing. Morgan James is a trademark
of Morgan James, LLC. www.MorganJamesPublishing.com

The Morgan James Speakers Group can bring authors to your live event. For more
information or to book an event visit The Morgan James Speakers Group at
www.TheMorganJamesSpeakersGroup.com.

ISBN 9781683500964 paperback
ISBN 9781683500988 eBook
ISBN 9781683500971 hardcover
Library of Congress Control Number:
2016916859

Cover Design by:
Rachel Lopez
www.r2cdesign.com

Interior Design by:
Chris Treccani
www.3dogdesign.net

In an effort to support local communities, raise awareness and funds, Morgan James
Publishing donates a percentage of all book sales for the life of each book to
Habitat for Humanity Peninsula and Greater Williamsburg.

Get involved today! Visit
www.MorganJamesBuilds.com

DEDICATION

I dedicate this book to all the silent voices looking for something more. May this book bring you strength, courage, and beauty, and lead you to sing loud and clear the joy of your life. Gain your Authoritative Control, break out of your prison and have the life you desire and deserve.

CONTENTS

Book Three - Focus

Book Four - Purpose

Your Next Steps…

FOREWARD

Do you realize that you, I, and everyone else on this planet are swimming in an ocean of infinite possibility? At every moment, we are surrounded by opportunities for wealth, health, happiness, success—anything and everything we want in life.

Unfortunately, very few people do realize this. Even fewer act on that realization.

When I first met Alena Chapman, she had a fire in her belly and a big dream. It was almost as if she'd heard the extraordinary opportunities and possibilities knocking at her door, threw it open, and said to them emphatically and without hesitation, "YES!" She knew she knew.

The book you are holding in your hands right now is the manifestation of the dream Alena shared with me that day. And it is a stunner.

The fact is, we are physically freer than we have been at any time in history. We can drive across town in minutes . . . fly halfway around the world in just a few hours . . . send messages to people virtually anywhere on earth that they receive in a heartbeat. And yet the most important freedom of all—inner freedom, the freedom to imagine and create the life one truly wants—is in dangerously short supply in most peoples' mind.

Alena calls it a prison. She is absolutely right. And what she offers within these pages are thoughts, ideas, and truths powerful enough to smash through the greatest obstacles to that freedom. I've witnessed it countless times, in countless lives, including my own. The truth is, the freedom to design your life exactly the way you envision it is NOT in short supply and is available to anyone who dares dream.

Alena Chapman has done the world a phenomenal service by delving deeply into her journey from self-imposed imprisonment to true freedom; by reflecting on the lessons she learned through the course of that journey; and by sharing those lessons with such courage and purpose. It is an honor and privilege to lend my voice to what I know will have people worldwide proclaiming the virtues and life-changing power of this wonderful book.

Absorb the wisdom and insight Alena reveals in the pages that follow. Follow the suggestions she puts forth to the letter, and you will do so much more than tear down the walls of whatever prison you find yourself in today. You will discover the power to build a life with the most spectacular and limitless view you can imagine. A life you are totally and completely in love with and one that is deserving of you.

Bob Proctor, Bestselling author of *You Were Born Rich*

ACKNOWLEDGMENTS

offer sincere thanks to:

Bob Proctor for his guidance and support in making my desire my reality.

Peggy McColl for her guidance and always finding time to help me during my new journey.

Scott and Ric Frishman of Jason and Morgan Publishing, Steve Harrison, Jack Canefield, Martha Bullen and Debra Englander who helped me reach higher and deeper to write this book. Nancy Crowe and Rachel Schuster for editing and clarity to bring this book and these special tools to millions.

My family and friends for their love, support, and keeping me real. All of you who are ready to say, "Enough is enough," and are ready for your dreams to be fulfilled. ix

BACKGROUND STORY

The sun felt so warm on my skin as it shined through the windshield of my car. The contrast of the deep blue sky and green trees was breath taking. I was astonished I did not feel gratitude for this beautiful day. Had I given away that much of myself that I could not feel blessed? Where had life gone so terribly wrong?

From deep inside myself I heard a soft voice say, "Enough is enough! It is time to be happy again. It is time to love your life." This voice seemed to rise up until finally I was saying it out loud to myself, the universe and to God. This was my wake up call.

I made a firm decision to be happy – to create a happy life. This was a burn the bridge behind me type of decision. I was not going back to the isolation, boredom, hurt and confusion that I had suffered in the last ten years. I had given parts of myself away and instead became and did what others felt was right. Soon I was unsure of my life and my purpose. Yes, I was a mother and a wife. Although I loved my family, it wasn't enough for me.

The decision was made and my life was about to change. I was going to be happy.

The Universe had heard my cry because the very next day books, messages and people would enter my life teaching me the "tools" to create my happiness. As I became happier, my marriage became worse. I wasn't fitting in the box that had held me for years. This caused the marriage to spiral downward and into divorce.

Although I wanted it to be easy and between my soon-to –be-ex and myself. Instead it became a four and a half-year very hard divorce. Although at first I was getting caught up in the mess I was presented with on a daily basis, the Universe kept putting mentors and messages that gave me the "tools" to not only survive the divorce, but thrive.

The "tools" helped me to gain clarity and vison for the future. I was able to focus on what was the benefit of all and not get weighed down with the attacks. These "tools" gave me the power to forgive even when things were at their worst and instead I was able to transcend and focus on what was the best for my children and myself.

Yes, there were times I became very upset. But because of these "tools" in time, I could gain perspective again.

I met four other women from around the United States enduring the same type of divorce that I was enduring. After four and a half years I was the only one who still had my children, my home and my life. I was the only one out of the five of us to mend the fence in our family so that our children feel good about both their father and their mother. And most of all I feel free to move on in my life. I am free from the anger and hurt. Instead my ex and I work together for the benefit of our children without hostility. I wish the very best for him.

It sounds like a fairy tale. I assure it is not.

Many people find themselves in a prison. It can be a prison of marriage, divorce, job or themselves. The choices we make in dealing with and escaping from our prison creates who we are and where we will go in our lives. Using the "tools" I was given provided me the option to see the choices and to choose wisely. I was able to distance myself from whatever was happening and instead focus on what was important.

It can be scary to leave our comfort zone or to find ourselves in a prison without an easy way out. Fear can take hold of us. The voices in our head saying, "Are you crazy! What are you doing? What if I fail? What if I can't succeed?" These voices crowd our thoughts and often times cause us to make the wrong choice for ourselves and those around us.

Close your eyes and breathe. Imagine feeling strong, happy and having inner peace. How does it feel? Do your shoulders relax? Do your stomach muscles loosen? Did you begin to smile? It is all very possible and closer to you than you think.

Open yourself up to the "tools" I have learned. Take a leap of faith. What do you have to lose? If nothing works you can go back to dealing with life the way you were before. Or maybe you can't! You may become aware enough of your own power, confidence and ability. Your dreams may be coming to you every day, beckoning you to "go for it." You may even begin to trust your own intuition and decisions without relying on other opinions. You will know what is right for you and you will have the strength to act on that inner knowing. You may laugh more. You may even find yourself dancing when no one is looking – the joy will be too much to hide. Your light will shine bright for all to see and admire. Life may become a miraculous journey.

It all has to do with the decisions you make.

"The Prison Effect" offers you these amazing tools along with concepts, insights and exercises that I have learned in order to break free from my prison of divorce and bloom into the person I wanted to be in the process. With each chapter you will find your strength, desire, compassion and confidence to change your life in the best way. You will benefit from my experience and the experiences of hundreds of others that I have helped achieve their own success and happiness.

This book offers you discovery of your own possibilities and abilities along with a way to make them your reality.

Are you ready to gain purpose? Are you ready to be happy? Are your ready to feel confident in the decisions you alone decide? Are you ready to rise above any mess, to see above the trees and gain the focus and vision to benefit not only yourself but all involved? Are you ready to fulfill your dreams and desires? And most of all, are you ready to take the step out of your prison and start to live? Now is your time.

I believe in the true you. I know you have what it takes and you will succeed.

There is a beautiful light inside you. This light has been hiding. Now is the time to allow this light, your light to grow, bloom and guide you. It contains all your strength, creation compassion, understanding and knowing. Shine it bright and feel absolutely free.

The beginning of your world is right inside this book. What are you waiting for?

If you would like to learn more about me, feel free to go to alenachapmanlife.com or join me on FB at Alena Chapman Twitter and Instagram is alena_chapman.

CHAPTER 1

Stepping Out of Chaos:

Authoritative Control

*It is an immense feeling of accomplishment
and freedom. You gain confidence and trust yourself.
You even love the person you have become.*

The very first "tool" the Universe presented me with was the tool of control. Actually, it was learning the difference between what I now call Phantom Control and Authoritative Control. What is the difference between these types of control and how do I fit into the picture, was the lesson that led me forward on my journey.

There is a principle in modern psychology called the "the locus of control." Where we are in this locus of control defines our tendency to assign responsibility to either internal or external causes for the various circumstances we find ourselves living.

There are two domains that people tend to gravitate towards to manage control in their lives. One is the external locus of control. People who use external locus of control tend to look for outward causes, responsibility or blame for things that are happening in their life. An example of this would be if I took a test at school and failed. It would not be my fault but instead the instructor did not teach the subject correctly or I was pushed on time with the test. Every reason for my failing would be outside of me. The opposite category is the internal locus of control, where a person tends to look inwardly to find their own measure of responsibility or control. Using the example of my failed test, an example of internal locus control would be that I look inside myself as to why I failed. Maybe I didn't study the right material or did not spend enough time studying. All the reasons would be because of something I did or did not do.

Everyone uses a little of both sides of the locus of control. The problem comes when either of these sides become extreme.

When we operate dominantly from an external locus of control we can fall into a pattern of what I call circumstantial blame. Circumstantial blame is where we habitually and automatically look for external forces upon which we can assign blame in order to absolve ourselves of any responsibility for our actions and our own circumstances. Using the example of a failed test, this would be the case if I kept failing the tests in school but considered none of it my fault. I would blame the teacher. Maybe she/he hates me or she/he is a terrible teacher or the tests weren't about what we learned. Every reason is not my fault; it is someone else's fault.

The problem with extreme external locus of control is the problem is apart from me. If it is the fault of someone else, then the responsibility to fix the problem lays with that person. I do not have the power or the control to be able to fix my own situation or problem.

However, if we operate dominantly from an internal locus of control we can fall into a pattern of self-blame. This means we habitually and automatically find ways to hold ourselves responsible and accountable even if, in fact, we are not responsible. We also tend to beat ourselves up for every little thing that goes wrong in our lives. If I had been studying very hard every night and weekend and still received grades I was not happy with, I would call myself stupid and begin studying even harder. I would feel badly about myself and push myself until I received a good grade. Even then I am not totally happy with myself or my ability. There is always something more I need to do to prove my worth to myself.

When we are in either an extreme pattern of external or internal locus of control we begin to recognize that we have actually lost control or things are not getting better. That feeling of loss of control is a state of chaos. Chaos feels unstable and unsure. So we reach into our bag of tricks looking for tools to give us some sense of control. The problem is that often, the only tools we think we have at our disposal are: worry, doubt, fear, stress, anxiety and more self-blame. When we stress over a situation it gives us this perverted sense of contribution, which gives us a minute feeling of a measure of control.

So whether we are in a state of self-blame or directing fault to someone else, we really are in a state of what I call Phantom Control. This is a state where we use anything at our disposal to manufacture a sense of control or contribution over a situation – when, in fact, any control that we conjure up is not real but a false sense that can sustain us for an extended period of time.

Many women and men in unhappy marriages will go to great extremes to stay away from each other. Each will blame the other for their unhappiness or the problems with the marriage. They will work separate jobs, have separate friends. If they must be together it is always in public, where they do not have to converse, or with their children, with whom they can converse. Anything so long as they are not together and can

Personal Control Blueprint

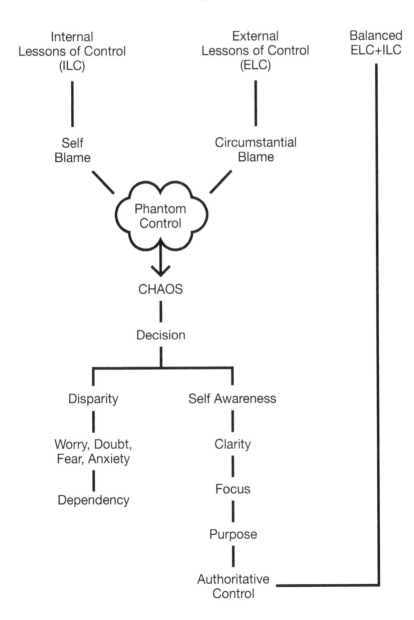

pretend everything seems fine and not their fault. But the marriage is still dispiriting; nothing has really changed. When the couple does come together, whatever their conflict is presents itself. The façade is broken. Anger, hurt, utter frustration and a feeling of chaos fills their hearts and minds. No one knows what to do to fix the situation.

This is when many fall into a state of complete despair. They have lost what control they thought they had by blaming and pretending and do not know what to do or where to turn.

The state of chaos is actually where we need to make a decision -- a decision that could determine the rest of your life. As I sat in my car feeling my lack of control, unhappiness and chaos, I made my decision. I wanted to be happy. I wanted a happy life. I would not settle for anything less.

I did understand it was a consequential time that could change my life if I allowed it. However, many do not realize this and instead cling to their phantom control, which leads to enduring physical and mental exhaustion and soon moves into despair. From despair, people look for relief or at least something to numb the pain and chaos. And this leads to dependency on outside substances such as alcohol or drugs – prescription or illegal.

Understanding this moment of chaos and knowing how important this time of decision is will be the key. Knowing what is in your heart, what you really want, is also important. This helps us to take another road. This is the road of learning, and growth. This is a state of what I call Self-Awareness and typically requires support, guidance or mentorship and persistence. However, it is the most rewarding and freeing path.

My road took much persistence; however, it was so very worth every twist and turn. I am amazingly happy. I have happy and achieving children. We might seem like we live in an ivory tower, but really we have made a choice to be happy, supportive, loving and respectful for each other. This took a decision, learning, acceptance and growth.

Where are you on the locus of control? Have you reached the Phantom Control, the chaos? If you have, and have picked up this book, then you have chosen a path of awareness, clarity, focus and finally Authoritative Control. Authoritative Control is the state where you authentically control your own circumstances regardless of any external factors that used to disrupt your life. You do not blame others nor do you blame yourself excessively. You see the circumstances for what they are, accept, surrender and move on in a way that is best for you and those around you. It is an immense feeling of accomplishment and freedom. You gain confidence and trust yourself. You even love the person you have become. Most important you know you can achieve anything you set your mind to and you can conquer any challenge that presents itself to you. Life is the joy, discovery and fun you always dreamt it would be.

Reaching Authoritative Control starts with a firm decision for what you want in your life. I wanted happiness and a life full of happiness. This decision moves you to the next step of awareness, where you begin to see your situation in its truth. The third step is gaining clarity for yourself. You begin to understand your strength, ability and confidence. Focus follows because you are understanding your possibilities and seeing the opportunities to unfold. Finally, there is purpose. Knowing what is in the best interest for you and all those you love. You have direction and the faith to know it will happen. These are the steps to Authoritative Control and becoming the Master of your life.

Open your mind and heart. Allow yourself to learn about you, your hurt, your feelings of not feeling whole or complete. Allow yourself to explore your strength, love and possibilities. We really owe ourselves and those we love our very best. Now let's begin the journey to uncover that very best.

Take Time to Focus:

1. Study the model of Locus to Focus BluePrint. Be honest with yourself. Where do you see yourself at this time? This is your starting point.

2. Challenge yourself to open your mind and heart to achieving the best in you. Allow yourself to read this book carefully, follow the exercises and develop discipline to form the habits and learn the tools for yourself.

3. If you have a friend who is also interested in taking this path of awareness and growth then, do this together. It is always great to have a person to talk to, to help in exploring and staying accountable. If there is not a friend, don't worry. You will gain one before this is over. Like always draws like.

AFFIRMATION: I, *(insert name)*, open my heart and mind to learn, discover, celebrate and love me. I make the decision to create a better, happier life. There is no stopping me now.

Date: _____

BOOK ONE
Awareness of Self

We are here to awaken from the illusion of our separateness.
THICH NHAT HANH

.

CHAPTER 2

Our Eyes are Open:

Acceptance

True awareness is awareness of our possibilities,
ability, capability to change any situation into
whatever we want it to be.

The ultimate truth is we have the ability to be, do and achieve anything we truly desire. Each one of us has Divine Source running through us. We are connected to something so much bigger than ourselves. This time is our time to shine.

Not having the awareness of this powerful truth handicaps us from achieving our full potential. Each challenge or obstacle weighs us down, instead of teaching and propelling us forward in our growth. Every day seems hard instead of waking to blessings, beauty and true abundance. We allow outside circumstances and situations to affect how we feel and what we decide. We give our light and power away.

Each "tool" I bring you in this book helped me to come closer and closer to the awareness of, what I like to call, the ultimate truth. Your starting point is when you accept this powerful truth and where you are at this present time, with all your present circumstances, problems or triumphs. Knowing you have greatness flowing through you gives you the ability to take this moment, accept it for what it is, learn the lessons it brings to you and move forward to a better situation.

The simplest definition of awareness is "knowing and understanding… about what is happening in the world around us." However, awareness of our possibility, growth and capability to change any situation into whatever we want it to be is the ultimate truth.

Sound a little hard to believe?

Why? Life is made up of the choices we make and what we believe about ourselves and our world. If I accept and feel in my heart that greatness of Divine Source runs through me and you, that I am full of possibilities and that I am part of something so much bigger than myself than I shape my decisions, actions and my life on this belief. If I feel that I do not deserve better, that life is hard and everyone is out to get me, that will be my reality. It will shape my life by how I respond and act and see everyone and everything I come in contact with every day.

There is your first choice. How would you like to live today – full of possibility or full of lack?

It really is that simple. And no, it does not depend on how bad the circumstance you are dealing with is at this moment. However how you are thinking, what you believe in your heart will determine how long you will remain in your bad circumstance or whether it will get worse or better.

Sounds simple, so what is the problem?

I had made a decision to break out of my feelings of isolation, hurt, anger to discover happiness and possibilities. I believed in my heart that it was possible to become that girl who once said "watch me" to any impossibility. The circumstances that came into my life gave me the opportunity to find and prove that I am that girl of achievement and happiness. I can honestly say that I would not have changed a single lesson because these lessons not only taught me but forced me to look inside myself and find that inner beautiful light. My light of strength, compassion, greater knowing and understanding. Once I found my light and shined it brightly my difficult circumstances began to change to opportunities.

There was a time in my life when two very difficult circumstances entered my life at the same time. Whether they were related or not is not for me to say and really doesn't matter. The first circumstance was my long, eye opening divorce after a marriage of 12 years. Divorce is never fun. Lawyers can be cruel and the process of divorce is invasive and sometimes insulting. The person you have loved, maybe had children with and built your whole world around has vanished. In their place is a person you do not know nor understand.

As I grieved the life disappearance of the life I knew and dealt with the normal hard and time-consuming divorce procedure another circumstance entered my life. These series of events seemed to appear out of nowhere and were making life very hard for my children and our family. Every day, sometimes two or three times a day, something would occur to scare us. Men lurking in the woods behind the house watching our every move, or being followed by not one but six cars. This excessive amount of cars may be because I do change my mind on direction when driving. One time I even was escorted out of town by two police and one sheriff car. I remember calling my attorney and saying, "You would think I was Princess Diana with all this attention."

To come to terms with these two difficult circumstances can feel overwhelming. At first I was shocked. How was I going to deal with all of this at once? Why was this happening? All I wanted was to be happy and have a life full of happiness? What was the Universe thinking?

As both circumstances grew more stressful and scary, I was discovering I had to make choices from inside myself. I had to rely on what I believed, not what was happening. When I began to do this, things began to change.

We all have times in our lives that are very difficult. When these times hit, it is hard to admit that the life we have worked so hard to create and always believed was the right way to live is now falling apart. The dream job has turned into a nightmare. The fairy-tale wedding doesn't have the happy ever after. The divorce doesn't want to go smoothly and quickly. Although everything we know is falling apart, it is actually an opportunity to change. How we want to change is our choice.

Unfortunately, many people I observe tend to close their eyes and proceed as if nothing is changing. They use their choice to pretend that everything is fine, the problems will disappear and life will get back to normal. In other words, many people choose denial as their solution to tough circumstances.

The problem with denial is that it shuts off all our inner senses. Our mind doesn't seem to notice the tension we feel in our shoulders and stomach. Our focus is cloudy and our thoughts jump from one idea to another without much clarity or understanding. We become scared to look too closely at ourselves or be alone with our thoughts because the wall of denial may come down and we would see what really is happening. So we keep very busy and accomplish little.

I could have closed my eyes to everything going on. I could have refused to see the cars driving by our home seven to eight times a night or the fear my children felt walking down the street to a friend's house. But what would the cost be? What would have happened if I pretended that everything was normal or worse, decided to hide in depression, drugs or alcohol? What would have happened to my children? What would I have lost?

A client friend found out just how costly denial can be. Lena found it easier to sneak drugs and drink than to deal with the attacks her divorce seemed to throw at her. Every morning before work she would either get high or drunk. Anything to help her deal with the loss of her marriage, a hard divorce and losing her life as she knew it. Lena stayed in this alcoholic comfort zone until she lost her children and her home in the divorce. The court deemed her to be too unstable to have custody.

Instead of going further into denial or pity, Lena took this wake-up call. She decided to call me.

As we worked to accept all the hurt, doubt and fear and start to understand, forgive and let go, Lena began to gain back her confidence and strength. Slowly but very steadily Lena created her life. She started to better the relationship between herself and her children. Then Lena took a quantum jump and started on a longtime dream of hers. She registered as student in a university to train as a teacher.

By the time Lena had her degree and a job teaching second grade, she was feeling great about herself and her life. It was time to get her children back. The court agreed to hear her case on custody and she was able to get joint custody of her children.

We are an ever growing and evolving energy/soul. We grow by the lessons we learn in this world. If we close our eyes to what is happening, we lose that chance to learn. Yes, sometimes the lessons are very hard. I can truly say four and a half years of my lesson seemed very long. However, it took me time to learn and then to practice and see the result of what I learned really work. If it had been shorter, it would have been a relief, but I am not sure I would have totally understood the power of my own light, my inner world and transcending or gaining a bigger perspective.

Once we lift the veil of denial, we can see where we are in our lives. It is like taking a reality check. We then accept where we are right now and know in our heart this is not where we need to stay. This provides us with the power to make a choice. What do we want to do from this moment forward?

We must open our eyes to our situation and understand that we are never truly trapped in a prison. We always have a choice. Gaining the awareness is allowing ourselves to see the choice or choices.

Denial is our ego creating a protective illusion for us. We see only what we want to see and we protect ourselves from anything we don't understand or feel we can't change for the better. Denial creates the feel-good illusion that does not allow us to see with clarity and change for the better.

My mother used to say that "nothing will happen to you that you cannot handle." I like this much better than the other saying I hear from people, which is, "What doesn't kill you makes you stronger." Again, your choice of belief. Either way we cannot become stronger or conquer the circumstance/difficulty if we close our eyes to it. Most important, we cannot grow.

So open your eyes! Take a good look with the thought that this is only temporary. It is your opportunity to learn the lesson, grow and move forward in a positive direction that makes you happy.

Some people feel that they have their eyes open, they understand they have a choice but still can't seem to move out of whatever is their problem. They just keep dealing with the circumstance without learning and achieving better. Why? Because there is an old belief holding back. It is something they learned long ago that is not serving them now. We call these old beliefs paradigms.

How do paradigms keep us stuck in unhappiness?

Sandy has said more times than not how she hates her life. She is not happy with her marriage. When I suggest to try a marriage counselor, she simply says, "That will not work." Instead of choosing to change something to better her life, she decided to stay in her known comfort zone and complain until her husband grew tired of her and found someone else.

I cannot begin to tell you how often I hear from people in all walks of life, "I hate my life." When I suggest they should change whatever they are not happy with in their lives, ninety-five percent of the time they reply they can't. Then they list excuses why changing their lives is impossible.

Why when we are faced with circumstances we do not want or enjoy, and we have the awareness that are lives are not serving us, do we choose to do nothing?

Some say it is laziness that keeps people from striving for better. I do not think this is totally true. After working with many people from different walks of life, I find that they do not see the vision or possibility that life could be exactly what they want it to be. They don't feel in control of themselves or their situation. Or they believe the lie that life is hard, unfair and you just have deal with your "lot your given" in life.

It is with these old beliefs or what is often called a paradigm, that we are not in control, that causes some to give up, suffer from anxiety or depression or even go past the unhappy stage to numbness. Instead of trying to change their situation, they simply go through the motions of their life feeling nothing. They become silent voices. Thus nothing changes except feelings of emptiness.

If I had allowed my paradigm of fear of these people who tried so hard to scare us, control my thinking or felt that everything was outside my control, then my children and I would have felt helpless. Instead I wanted my children to feel safe. I could not control the people who wanted to get into my house; however, I could make it as difficult as I possible. I learned better ways to protect my home. I installed garage bolts and used bars across the doors at night. Everything was well protected. Taking those steps helped me to feel more capable of taking care of myself and my family. It empowered me and allowed me to feel good about the choices I was making.

Opening our eyes and recognizing that we are allowing a paradigm to rule our life is a huge awareness. The more you conquer this paradigm the more you are free from it! It will not rule your decision-making ever again. There are many ways to change our paradigms. The key is to realize we have the power to believe what is true for us. We can change any thought that does not help us create the life we know we deserve.

As a Man Thinketh by James Allen and even the Bible, state in one form or another: What we believe in our heart is what will become our life. We are what we believe and our lives are what we believe.

If a paradigm is keeping you in a life of unhappiness, boredom or anger…look at what you believe about yourself and your world. You are a very powerful being. You are an amazing light. There is no boundary on what you can achieve. Your inner light is for ever greater expansion and expression. Anything that holds you back from that can be changed.

When we have the strength and desire to step outside our box or situation it is an amazing feeling. You do have control of your life. You can make a huge difference in any situation you are confronted with in your life. The more steps you take the more empowered you feel. It is simply taking that very first step!

Friends and family sometimes keep us stuck

Even if some people have the desire to move forward and better their circumstance, some will lack the courage of facing criticism of friends and family.

Often when you finally realize you must change your life, family and friends will rush to provide you with all the reasons why you can't change. As more and more incidents began to occur, friends and family rushed to tell me how I should have never gotten a divorce. It was too dangerous to be alone. Did I realize what I was causing my family to go through?

It takes awareness that staying in the situation is worse than starting something new. It is an awakening to what is possible. Once we see what our lives could be like, it is hard to keep allowing ourselves to live day to day in an unhappy situation even when others try to keep us there. Courage to stand up to the comments and criticism can be easy if you believe in where you want to take your life.

Yes, I could have stayed in a loveless marriage, feeling miserable and isolated. But how would that affect my children and their future relationships? Would they marry into the same situation? How would they understand what true love is like? Didn't I, as the parent, owe them a better example or at least show them happiness? I knew in my heart they needed to understand better.

When a person decides to change his or her life, it is because something has clicked. An event, thought, or word has broken through the paradigm or the denial and the true issue cannot be ignored anymore.

Now that my awareness of my situation was known I must choose how I want to move forward. With our home protected it was time for a family meeting. We need to move forward together. I also decided that from this point on I would try to stay above the mess and keep my eye on my purpose – to make this divorce as smooth as possible for my family and for all of us to be happy.

As we choose to break free and create the lives we want to live, we have a decision. We can proceed to break free through the illusion that the problem is with someone or something other than us. This is very easy, but it's still denial. Nothing can truly become better if you refuse to take the power back into your own hands.

The Ultimate Awareness

So we have opened our eyes to the truth of our situation, to the influences that may be keeping us stuck, but what makes us want to step out of our box – to become more

I think everyone must know, deep down inside, there is something better. Life is a gift. We have a purpose. It is time to believe in our dreams, ourselves and our own ability.

How do you see the life you want to live? What is your desire? Even if you are unsure what you want, you must want better? You want to feel happy and love getting up in the morning to start the day. You may want to feel immense gratitude for all the gifts life has to offer? You may wish to feel free – totally free. Is this possible? It most certainly is.

Deciding to take that first step out of your unhappy comfort zone is not only possible but necessary. Deciding to read this book, practice with the exercises and gain awareness of your own is an excellent first step.

We are on a journey about you, your dreams, and your future. To do this we must also learn the lessons of the past, forgive and let go. We must see with clarity and gain strength, confidence and vision for moving on.

You have the awareness that there is more to life or that you are unhappy with your current situation. You have picked this book to read for a reason. You are on the journey to something better. I congratulate you.

No one was put on this earth for the purpose of living in a situation that makes someone miserable. On the contrary, we were born to be happy. It is time to gather your courage to break through and live it.

The time is now!

Take Time to Focus:

1. Get yourself a journal or pad of paper. It can be your workbook to help discover you. Start by describing your life situation. Write it as objectively as you can – this means without much emotion. This can help you look at all the facts. Then write why you feel you are stuck or in a prison.

2. Become aware of when you are happy. Where are you and what is happening when you are happy? What are you happiest doing?

Write what is making you happy and why. How often do you get to do things that make you happy?

3. Take a walk in nature. Feel the energy and listen to the peace that surrounds you. This is reality. This is beauty. Be very grateful and allow your mind to quiet.

4. Sign the affirmation on the when you are ready. There is an affirmation after each chapter. You sign it when you are ready to take the step or learn the lesson each chapter presents. The affirmation is a promise you are making to yourself, so sign it only when you are ready. Read it every morning and night.

AFFIRMATION: I, (*insert name*), as have decided that _____(*insert date*) enough is enough. I will no longer endure a life I am not happy living. I deserve to be happy. From this point on I will take the steps and learn the lessons I need to break free from my prison and gain my freedom. It is my life and I want to live it.

Date: _____

CHAPTER 3

Your World Awaits!

Possibility

Conformity is thought of as safe,
normal, and acceptable,
but it carries a price for personal growth
and the growth of society

magine waking every morning happy, a little excited and jumping out of bed to start your day. You feel in control of you and your life. You have your eyes wide open to opportunities and possibilities. Life is a fantastic adventure.

Sounds like a fairy tale, but it is not. It takes claiming your authoritative control.

What is authoritative control? It is accepting who and where we are in the present moment and who we want to be in our future. It is understanding that mind, body, and soul are not separate parts of us, but parts of the whole. It is making sure we grow in every part of our lives and being.

Authoritative control is knowing we are in control of our happiness, our perception of our world, and how we choose to respond.

My very first mentor taught me about taking control of me and the importance of acceptance. It is one thing to open our eyes and gain awareness of our situation; the next step is to say, "Okay, this is where I am right now. This is who I am right now." Now we have a choice. "What do I want our life to look like? Who do I want to be as a person?" Once we begin to accept ourselves and our lives at the present time, we can begin to move forward with clarity and focus.

The journey of discovery is ever-evolving. Sometimes we need to heal from past hurts, anger, or betrayal. Other times we have to break through the old beliefs/paradigms that keep us from growing and achieving in our lives. The best part is that we are taking control for our growth.

Freedom comes with accepting that only you can make or break you. When I made the decision to love my life again, I was not asking others if it was okay. I was saying, "Enough is enough. I am going to take back control of me, look for the opportunities, get beyond any barriers, and start loving my life." I was taking responsibility and control for myself and my happiness. It was the first important step in my journey.

When we take authoritative control we begin to steer our boat in the direction we want to go. It is an exciting feeling to know I can be the master of my life. I may listen to others opinions however, I am the one who decides and I am the one responsible for who I want to be. This is tremendously freeing because by acknowledging this I am taking responsibility for my thoughts, responses, and habits.

Nothing outside of me controls me. I always have a choice and my choice designates how I want to grow as a person and where I want to go.

It really is an amazing realization. After all this is not what we are taught in school.

The terms control and responsibility seem to scare many away.

I have noticed how the words "responsibility" and/or "control" seem to cause so many people to cringe. It's a funny side effect of society's value of conformity or fitting in.

My children used to go to a school which requires students to wear a uniform. The parents loved the simplicity of everyone wearing the same thing. The students were forever trying to find ways to show their individuality even if that meant sneaking on some funky colored socks. The conformity did not stop with clothing. Everything in the curriculum confined the students to a certain way of thinking. Discussions were based on what the school allowed, problem solving was permitted only within the terms the teachers allowed, and leadership could happen only under the terms set by the school. Thinking outside the box, creative problem solving, and individuality were not encouraged, but instead tightly controlled.

Conformity is thought of as safe, normal, and acceptable, but it carries a price for personal growth and the growth of society. If we conform to what society deems appropriate for us, we give up authoritative control of ourselves. Individually exploring the questions of our purpose on the planet, how our special gifts can better the world, and how we can achieve peace and happiness are bypassed altogether. Many feel it is too hard to be what they feel is different from people around them. Some are scared of what they may find if they look inside themselves. Others who have lived only in conformity may not understand there is another way to live. Lives based on conformity become rote, boring, and sometimes meaningless.

We even praise children for pushing their dreams away to keep the parents' dreams alive. Many parents encourage their children to be lawyers/doctors/bakers because they are lawyers/doctors/bakers. I can't imagine telling my children they must live the dream I choose for them. It really seems ridiculous.

I grew up in a very traditional religious family. We believed whatever the man on the pulpit said. This all worked fine as long as we didn't want to think any further — and as long as the problems of life never led us to question what we were being told.

My marriage was in serious trouble for at least six years before we decided to divorce. People who are divorced in my religion were and sometimes still are ostracized and made to feel as if they committed a serious sin. I grew up watching a brave divorced person walk up to take communion with her arms folded across her chest only to receive a blessing because her sins were too great to permit her to receive the host. The entire congregation watched. The message was loud and clear: Don't divorce. If you were in an unhappy marriage, you were supposed to endure and pretend everything was normal. I was once told by an aunt on my ex-husband's side of the family that "no one is really happy. Life is too hard. Happiness really doesn't exist."

Does True Happiness Exist?

True happiness does exist, but to receive it, you need to take responsibility and achieve authoritative control and decide to be happy. Authoritative control is understanding we are the only ones who can determine our world. It is up to us to define what and who we are, to heal ourselves, and to grow in our awareness and abilities. It is up to us to find our gifts, compassion, and strengths. It is up to us to decide if our present situation is right for us or not. The more we discover of ourselves the more we can give to others.

There is an old saying that "you can't give what you don't have." My ex-husband's aunt did not believe in happiness because she did not feel or have happiness in her world. She could not give what she did not have.

Authoritative control is caring for ourselves — listening to and respecting the body, learning to open our minds and train our thoughts, and nurture our spiritual life. It is gaining the awareness of our higher selves and being true to what this all means for our lives.

Some would call this selfishness. I feel that selfishness is expecting everyone to give up on themselves and their dreams simply to live what is considered "normal."

We need to understand that the concept of normal is not real. At a recent family gathering, someone asked what was wrong with living a normal life. I replied, "What constitutes a normal life?" Everyone stopped eating to look at me. "Does anyone really know a normal family or normal life?" I asked. Not one family member could think of a normal family or life.

When we have authoritative control or responsibility to ourselves we know that whatever we feel is normal for us is, indeed, normal. We understand what is right for us even if it isn't exactly what others call normal.

Each of us came to this wonderful planet to have experiences that help our energy and soul evolve and grow. We are part of the collective whole. I really think this is why, even though the danger of living without the group has disappeared, we still need others around us. If a person lives without anyone around except animals, then that person will become friends with the animals. We are social because we are all connected.

This connection does not mean we must stifle who we are or be what others think we should be. On the contrary, the more we open up to our inner selves, our dreams, desire, understanding and our love, we grow and become happy. Our inner self is all about expanding and expressing or growing and creating. This enables us to share that much more with the world around us in a positive and productive way.

This is what it means to live with ultimate freedom and independence. It is also the way we can strengthen our understanding and connection to others and opening our compassion and unconditional love. Imagine how our lives would be if everyone was happy and living to expand and express their inner-selves. No longer would anyone try to make anyone else live with fear or doubt. Better still, we would not feel constrained by criticism or fear. The freedom to live our lives to their very fullest and better our world would be achievable for everyone.

All I wanted was to love my life again and have that confident and happy girl back as me. I did not realize this desire would lead me on a journey of authoritative control of me and a life of doing what I love to do. However, after I made my decision and the opportunity to authoritative control came, I opened my heart and mind to receive it.

And there lies the key to growth. When opportunity knocks answer the door. Whenever a mentor came into my life I opened myself to them and learned. Learning responsibility for myself was a precious realization that has served me still. All I had to do was to graciously receive what I was being taught. This is also authoritative control.

When we decide to open ourselves to taking responsibility to achieve our authoritative control, we begin an amazing journey of discovery. It really is magical. Sometimes it may seem a little difficult, but the rewards are freedom and a life you love living. What could be better than that?

Take Time to Focus:

1. Allow time to sit and reflect. If you would like to meditate, great. As you relax, feel your heart open to receiving. Feel as it grows bigger, then open your mind in the same way. When you feel ready, say to the Universe: "I am READY. It is my time!"
2. Write out on one side of the paper where in your life you don't feel in control. Now on the other side of the paper write out ways you can be in control to each item you feel you are not in control.
3. If you have problems completing the first Take Time to Focus, rip out or write out the affirmation below. Tape it on a mirror and read it several times a day while looking into the mirror. First read it while looking into the right eye. Then read it as you look into

the left eye. Do this several times a day until you feel open and ready to receive all the blessings the Universe will bring you.

AFFIRMATION: I, (*insert name*) am ready to be responsible to self. I am ready to open my heart and mind to discovery, blessings, and opportunities. I want freedom to be me!

Date:_____

CHAPTER 4
Take Back Your Life:

Responsibility

*Enough is enough. I am the master of my fate
and the captain of my soul.
I will take the responsibility of
my actions and thoughts.*

heard a parent talking to their child of 11 years old. Their child was what seemed to be somewhat shy girl with glasses. The parent was scolding the child for sticking up for herself against a bully in her class who has been torturing her for the last three months. This shy eleven year old, seemed to have gathered her courage and strength and had given her attacker a bloody nose. The parent was horrified.

"If someone is bullying you, you mustn't fight back. If you do then you are the bully," she said very firmly.

My first thought was why are we teaching our children to be victims? I then, answered my own question. "Because we, ourselves have become victims."

We live in an age of victimhood. Nothing is our fault. If we lose our job it is the offices fault. If our relationship fails, it is because our spouse did not care enough or listen more or was too demanding. If we are fat, it is not our fault for eating too much. Instead it is the fault of large portions at restaurants, or easy fast food. We have become a society of victims.

Victimhood is a form of denial. If someone else or something else is at fault, then we do not have to take action. We are not responsible. This type of reasoning is a double edge sword. If I am not responsible then it follows, I am not in control of the situation. Everything is outside of my control.

And let's face it, being a victim creates sympathy. "He left me and I had no idea. Why would he do this to me?" Because the victim ego needs this narrow view in order to feel right, it must look outside itself for sympathy and validation. The problem is that victimhood mentality zaps our energy. And in order for us to keep the sympathy of friends and family we must relive the feelings of hurt/anger over and over. It becomes a vicious cycle.

It is important to note that each time we put the blame on someone or something apart from ourselves, we remove our ability to understand and learn from the circumstance, forgive and move on to a better place. Instead, we hold on to the anger which, over time, becomes bitterness. These negative feelings actually lodge in our muscles and other parts of our body.

At first I was angry. "Why was someone trying to scare me and my family? Why was it so important to scare my children? Why was all this happening during the divorce? Why was my soon-to-be-ex's lawyer being so insulting? He didn't know me." Everything felt out of my control. It was all happening to me. I was a victim.

Anger is a powerful energy. It creates the flight or fight syndrome in our bodies which activates our adrenal gland causing our muscles to tense, our stomach to tighten and our jaw to set. We are ready to strike or run. If this anger continues over a longer period of time our body continues to activate the adrenal gland and we stay tense. Our bodies are not made to stay in this way. That is when problems develop.

Anger and worry seem to be the two emotions/energies that cause fear, anxiety that lead to depression or other more serious ailments. As stated in a report by the *Journal of the American Medical Association* (JAMA), in 2015, the use of antidepressants in America rose from 6.8% to 13%.

The writing is on the wall. We as a society cannot rely on blame and allow ourselves to stay victims. It is not good for our emotional, mental or physical being. Throughout history we as a people have created and grown in our technology, science and ourselves. This is our spirit's purpose – greater expansion and expression. We have been innovators, creators and strong. When we stop and allow ourselves to feel stuck as we do as a victim, we are not allowing our truest self to grow.

To understand this a little better, let's go back to our 11-year-old girl. Just imagine if you were bullied for three months and finally gathered the courage inside yourself to say "Enough." You feel strong and able to take care of yourself. You now understand that you do not have to be afraid – you can do it. And then you are told that this is all wrong. You must stay feeling afraid, weak and not believing in your own strength and ability to solve the problem. You must rely on others to solve the problem, and they do not seem to be helping. Needless to say, that is a very scary place for a little girl.

There are bullies who can interrupt our life at any age. Mine were affecting my family. Just like the little girl dealt with her bully, I needed to deal with mine. I did not know who it was, but I could still protect myself and my family. Even more important was to stop being afraid of the big bad wolf. Anger and fear only cause more anger and fear. Once I made the decision to rise above the fear I knew in my heart that nothing dangerous was going to happen. This enabled me to deal with the situation with much more clarity and vision. I was not a victim anymore and this provided me with strength.

My question to you is why would anyone want to stay where they feel weak, unsure and incapable. Not being able to deal with a situation definitely creates worry, doubt and fear. No wonder antidepressants have gained so much popularity.

How do we break the vicious cycle of victimhood in our lives?

Let's start with being honest with ourselves. Yes, the restaurants may be giving us bigger portions; the pressure at the job may have been too much; and maybe our spouse really didn't care how we felt. However what role, other than victim, did we play in our circumstance? Look deeper. Did we have to eat all that food? What could we have done to lessen the pressure? Do we procrastinate or take on too much? And did we know before we got seriously involved with the non-caring spouse that he/she was indeed not a very caring person? What was our role?

This is the first step in taking responsibility for ourselves and our lives.

There is a poem by William Ernest Henley I read every morning and every night. It empowers me and reminds me I am in control of me.

Invictus

Out of the night that covers me,
 Black as the pit from pole to pole,
I thank whatever gods may be
 For my unconquerable soul.

In the fell clutch of circumstance
 I have not winced nor cried aloud.
Under the bludgeonings of chance
 My head is bloody, but unbowed.

Beyond this place of wrath and tears
Looms but the Horror of the shade,
And yet the menace of the years
Finds, and shall find, me unafraid.

It matters not how strait the gate,
How charged with punishments the scroll.
I am the master of my fate,
I am the captain of my soul."

I am the master of my fate. You are the master of your fate. We are responsible for what paths we choose to take. We are responsible for who and what we allow into our lives. No one else is the master of our lives. No one else chooses our fate.

I am the captain of my soul. I alone know who my true self is. I know my true desires and only I can make my soul's desires a physical reality. We are all captains of our souls.

It takes responsibility to own our fate. It is our responsibility to listen to our souls, our desires and our purpose. It is our responsibility to make the choices to create the lives we want to live. It is our responsibility to own our mistakes. Mistakes are not bad.

They actually allow us to learn what we don't want or what does not work. The best way to handle mistakes is to own them as yours, learn the lesson they teach, and let them go. Beating yourself up about a mistake almost always puts you back into a victim role.

I have authoritative control over my life and me. I always feel my life is like a giant ship and I am the captain. It is my job to steer my ship to the land or life I want to live. There may be storms, high waves, or even rocks, but I will steer my ship through them. I am the captain, the master of my fate.

I saw how my marriage friends, family, and even my lawyer—whether intentionally or not—put me in a victim role. "Look what they are doing to you," I often heard. But I was not a victim. I would not allow myself to be put in that role. Being a victim would not help me or my family move towards a positive life. I did not want to waste time, energy and all my focus on "poor me." I was responsible for my ship, and I alone was steering it towards a happier life.

Taking responsibility and claiming your authoritative control is very empowering. What a wonderful feeling it is to be in control of oneself. It helps you to believe in you. Why shouldn't you believe in you? Only you can steer your boat. By choosing to allow everyone and every circumstance to steer your boat, you are allowing everything else to pick your path. In the process you lose your direction and your true purpose.

I now know that it was the choices I made to not be a victim, to have responsibility of self and be proactive in forgiveness, purpose and rising above in meditation to see clearly that helped me keep perspective and sanity throughout the four and one half years. It was knowing I had the most influential power ever: Myself! No matter what happened I could control how I would respond to create better out of any situation. I, alone, was and still am, the captain of my ship.

We have the choice.

The saying "you sow what you reap" means whatever you do has a result. This is the Universal Law of Cause and Effect. If you choose to lose your temper and say something very hurtful, then you will suffer the consequence of the other person becoming angry and yelling hurtful things back to you. However, if you instead chose to say, "Let's take some time to calm down and discuss this a little later," you now have created a calmer, proactive situation which allows for understanding and growth. So it stands to reason, if I chose to stay in a situation that causes me to feel lost, sad and confused, then the result would be I would grow to become angry or depressed. If I chose to be a victim and feel the anger and helplessness, than I would always stay a victim and suffer the consequences. But if I took control over myself and what I could do to improve my situation, then I feel empowered, capable and my confidence and strength grows.

Understanding the Law of Cause and Effect and that God or the universe is filled with goodness, beauty, love, joy, and faith, leads you to understand that all hurt, sadness, anger, cheating, vengeance, and self-loathing are of our own making, not the universe's making. All our misery comes from within us. Love and joy are also within us. We create our conditions, because what we sow is what we reap.

Take back your power and claim your life.

If you truly want to change or break free from a situation in which you are unhappy, you need to say, "Enough is enough. I am the master of my fate and the captain of my soul. "No more complaining or giving negative energy to your situation. Instead, I will take the responsibility of my actions and thoughts." You are taking the first huge, positive step to improving you, your mind, and your situation.

From this point on there is no need for victimhood or complaining because you are steering your boat forward to better waters. Complaining or being a victim is an anchor that will hold you mentally and physically in place. You are moving on. Your whole being should now be looking within to find direction, happiness, and strength. You are ready to start your journey.

Take Time to Focus:

1. Read "Invictus" once or twice a day. Feel you are in control. You are the master of your fate. You are the captain of your soul. Say it with feeling.

2. Make two columns. In the first column write ways that you feel like a victim. In the second column write ways to not feel like a victim anymore.

3. Take a walk in the woods or a park. Whatever you find to feel peaceful, quiet and alone and reflect on the situation you are not happy with in your life. What was your part in this drama Try to look at it with more objectivity. There is no blame nor guilt. Now think about why it all happened the way it did? How could you have responded in a different way creating a different outcome?

4. After you have finished with your self-discovery in no. 3, now how do you want to proceed? It is your choice. How do you want to see yourself and what actions do you feel you should take to feel this way?

5. Read Chapter 4 and begin to understand even more and begin to heal.

AFFIRMATION: I, _(*insert name*), am the master of my fate, the captain of my soul. I am in control of me and I say, "Enough is Enough." I am ready to have a better life.

Date:_____

CHAPTER 5

Let It Flow:

Surrender

*We have perfection running through us
connecting us to a vast, incredible universe.
This universe is full of possibilities,
opportunities, and blessings.*

As you look back on your life, you may wonder: How did I manage to get so stuck in a life I am not happy living? How did I get so off the path I thought I was living? Why did I live in this prison for so long?

The one belief I hold fast to is that everything in our lives happens for a reason. The paths we take in our lives help us to grow physically and spiritually. My marriage was not perfect and I was not happy. However, I bore three beautiful children who are my world. Whatever was happening during my divorce has helped me to grow into a person of greater compassion, serenity, strength and wisdom. Would I be the same person if not for these events? No. Understanding the loneliness, frustration, anxiety, and anger of people living in their prison would have been a foreign concept to me. I would not have the compassion and wisdom to understand and help others to break free.

Acceptance of our past or present is looking at it realistically and saying, "It is what it is." Seeing our present as our starting point and trusting in Infinite Source/God/Universe is the path to growth of our higher selves.

Many call it divine guidance or the soul's path. Everything that occurs in our life is for the evolution of our soul/higher self. We have a purpose on this earth, and that is to evolve, expand, and grow spiritually. How we grow and the path we choose is free will. All paths lead to our spiritual growth, even if some paths are harder than others. This is important because if we understand that every road leads to the same end, we then never have to feel we took a wrong turn in life. We may have chosen a harder road, but even then, there were more lessons and who is to say that didn't help evolve your soul/energy even further.

Everything we choose in life is for the evolution of our soul. Understanding the connection we have with Source can influence whether we are making decisions with our higher or lower selves. Choosing our path based on hurt, fear, need, or addiction is choosing from our lower selves or the ego. The path most likely will lead to a harder life with more hurt, fear, or need. If we choose to accept where we are now, let go of the vengefulness, betrayal, and anger and instead understand what led us here, learn from our mistakes, and heal, we move forward with growth, strength, and guided wisdom. This is important. This wisdom comes from understanding that whatever path we choose, we are where we need to be in order to evolve.

Trusting in Source/God/The Universe is accepting "what is," learning from it and moving into our new cycle with faith that everything that happens will be for our purpose. As I dealt with my divorce, I gained more objectivity and was able to transcend the difficulties and open my eyes to better possibilities. If I had remained full of anger, vengefulness, hurt or fear, I would still be fighting in court today. I would have become bitter, hard, and unbending. By being objective, forgiving, surrendering and rising above, I was able to do what was best for the whole family and grow into the person I am now.

When we understand and believe how connected we are to the Universe and Source/God, trusting that everything will always be in our best interest is easy.

Connecting to our higher selves comes with meditation and acceptance. Through meditation we reach within to our higher self. This higher self is perfect. It is the connection to Source/God. We have perfection running through us connecting us to a vast, incredible universe. This universe is full of possibilities, opportunities, and blessings. It has everything our souls need for greater expansion and expression. There is no need for negativity or victimhood. You have so much more waiting for you.

Trusting myself and setting my intention for a life I loved living started me on my journey. Teachers and events began to enter my life. I still do not know how I met wonderful mentors — they simply seemed to appear in my life. I received and learned. Opportunities to share what I learned came when I was asked to teach with an organization through the court system. If couples going through a divorce or a single partner dealing with custody did not seem reasonable or were extremely bitter or angry, they were sent to my class. The classes were designed to help the participants see from a better perspective past anger, fear and hurt. Every person I worked with started changing their lives in positive ways. To this day I still see members of the class. I am always so happy to see how their lives have changed for the better in every way.

When I decided to keep a journal, little did I know I would meet an author right at my table in the coffee shop. This is divine guidance, or as I call it, Gifts of the Universe. Some call it synchronicity. This is when you find things happening that lead to things you want to happen and opportunities just appear out of now where – or so it may seem. It happens throughout your day. It is our choice to receive this guidance or to ignore it. If we are full of our own ego and negative emotions, we won't even see these gifts. In order to see we must accept, learn from it, and let it go. Then clarity will come.

Stacey struggled with the dismantling of her family through divorce. She had moved from a city she loved to the home town of her now ex-husband. All her friends and relatives were back in the city. Now she sat in a town she did not like, single and unhappy. When we spoke, I could see Stacey did not harbor any resentment or anger against her ex-husband. The major issue of her sadness stemmed from the fact that she had to live in the town so the children could see both parents. Second, she wanted to improve the relationship between the children and their dad.

Stacey was a sales manager with a major car manufacturer. I asked if that involved travel. It did, but Stacey usually opted out because she did not want to leave her children. The children did not want to spend time with their father, so she had them all the time.

As we worked together, Stacey began to accept that her life at this moment in time was where it needed to be. She then chose to learn from it and trust the universe as she planned how she wanted to move forward. She became calmer, more focused, and happier. Methods such as visualization helped her to see how she could talk to her children about their father in positive, uplifting ways.

One morning Stacey came to me very happy. "The children had a great time with their dad yesterday and I have come to a major decision," she said. "Once our children get very comfortable with their dad again — I give it about one month — I am going to ask my boss to allow me to start traveling for my job. The kids can stay with their dad the times I need to travel and I get to leave town for a little while. It really is perfect. Why didn't I see it before?" I explained the process of accepting had opened her heart and mind to thinking of solutions best for all involved. Accepting had allowed her to release any negative and instead, trust and transcend the situation, giving her clarity.

There is a reason we are in this point of our lives. There is a lesson we must learn so our soul/energy can grow and evolve. Stacey had to learn the importance of co-parenting and what was best for the children. By accepting this and trusting our Universe/Source, we open our eyes with clarity to our next move in our journey. Without this clarity or acceptance, we choose a road with more hardship or chaos.

It is an incredible feeling of calm and understanding. Worry, doubt, and fear are nonexistent. There is much more living in the present, being grateful, and enjoying life. Why would anyone want to live any other way? Why would we choose to feel long-lasting anger, vengeance, or negative feelings? We have a precious short time on this earth. Why not enjoy and make something great from it all?

Accept the now, trust in the future and enjoy the journey. Sounds easy — it is! We simply have to let go of our ego and get out of our own way. How do we learn to surpass the ego?

Ask yourself next time you have a decision to make, "Is this choice for the betterment of everyone involved or is this only for the betterment of my situation." If you choose for the betterment of all involved – congratulations. You have surpassed the ego to your higher, all knowing, visionary, compassion filled, true higher self.

To this day I still feel it was surrendering my situation, taking control where I could and allowing the divorce to unfold that helped me to keep all the events in life in perspective. I did not suffer from the fear that all my friends seemed to feel for me. I saw the bigger picture. This gave me a little bit of serenity and peace.

One of my favorite tools is meditation. Understanding, gaining clarity, new awareness, and having a safe place to explore the higher self all begin with meditation. The more we understand and experience our higher selves the easier it is to accept, forgive, and let go. We come to know when we are making decisions from our higher self or from our ego. Meditation is where transcendence begins.

Deepak Chopra describes this still place within us as "...the source of life.... One finds peace, harmony." In this perfect, unchanging part of ourselves, we find the "bliss" and begin to understand who we are, what our purpose is and what is important. When we take the time to quiet ourselves and find this special part of us, we begin to understand life.

Take Time to Focus:

1. Find time twice every day to talk to Infinite Source/God or the Universe. Allow yourself to feel close. Notice the beauty of the sky and feel Source. All day feel how you are surrounded and supported by this immense power and love of the Universe.

2. List your negative feelings. Now look back at the situation again. Are your feelings truly reasonable? Is the situation as bad as you previously thought?

3. Now describe what would be best for all involved. How you would like to see the situation resolve?

4. Begin to imagine how you can respond or act/do to do what is best for all involved.

5. How would you like to surrender your situation to Source? This is your own special moment. You may enjoy simply speaking with God/Source/Universe. Or you may like to write it out and burn it, surrendering it up. The choice is yours. Make it fun and special.

AFFIRMATION: I, *(insert name),* surrender myself, my desires and the "how" to the Universe. I trust and lift it all up to Infinite Source.

Date:_____

BOOK TWO
Clarity

Yesterday is a dream, tomorrow but a vision.

But today well lived makes every yesterday a dream of happiness, and every tomorrow a vision of hope. Look well, therefore, to this day.
—SANSKRIT PROVERB

CHAPTER 6

It is Time to Discover You!:

Meditation

Why meditation?
It is because everything seems crazy,
unknowing, and difficult.
Your mind is moving so fast,
skipping from one problem to the next

t is extremely difficult to gain clear perception or clarity when our minds are jumping from negativity to judgmental or anxiety ridden thoughts. You have to wonder are we ruling our thoughts or are our thoughts ruling us. Or if you are like me, you will receive ten ideas every minute. Your minds never stop.

Why do we want to quiet our minds? Because when our minds are quiet we find that place that some have said "is everywhere and nowhere."

It is the true self and it holds the clarity, calmness, love and compassion we cannot feel or hear when our mind is running a mile a minute or is filled with worry, doubt and fear.

So how do we begin to quiet our minds?

Actually, a great way to learn to quiet your mind is through meditation. When you meditate you begin to slow down the thinking. You do not stop the thinking. Instead, it simply focuses on something deep within. It begins focusing on feeling, hearing. It is amazing what you will hear and learn. Yes, I can hear you: "What? Quiet my mind when I am so eager to move forward? When my world might be turned upside down? Quiet my mind? Are you crazy?"

No, I am not crazy. It is because everything seems crazy, unknowing and difficult. Your mind is moving so fast, skipping from one problem to the next. When you quiet you and your mind through meditation you begin to gain a clearer understanding of your circumstance and about you. As you practice meditation you will find it to be a time that you will treasure, a time during which you will gain answers and become centered.

How to Begin

First, find a place that is only for you alone. A place you love and where you find yourself wanting to be. This can be a room, a corner of a room, a garden, church, out in nature or simply any place where you're comfortable and able to relax. Now, discipline yourself to find some time every day to sit in your special place. This is important! Schedule the same time every day or vary the time. The point is to never miss a day. This discipline begins to form a positive habit. It establishes a special time for you to discover you.

When you enter your area say, "No doubt, fear or worry enters here." Then proceed to sit in a comfortable position. If you are in nature, then close your eyes and listen to the sounds of nature. If you are inside, music or meditation tapes, bells, drums, or guided meditation can help. If you have not meditated before or have been in a negative environment, a guided meditation may be helpful to relax you and raise your vibration. Put the tapes on and sit, close your eyes, and listen. Allow yourself to follow the voice on the tapes. Become aware of your breath and make it go deeper and slower. Start to relax all parts of your body, especially areas where you hold tension like your shoulders, neck, legs, arms, and hands. Also relax the muscles in your face. Relax everything. Feel centered and whole. And simply enjoy and listen.

I was not one someone who could meditate. The idea of sitting with my legs crossed with perfect posture for what seemed like hours at a time was not my idea of a good time. For me it started with a walk in a tree-laden park. I was the only one there and could hear the birds sing, lulling me to quiet my thoughts and listen. This led me to find what I like to call "my spot." Many meditation and spiritual teachers stress the importance of having our own sacred spot. When you enter your spot, you feel safe to allow your mind and body to relax. I found my spot at an old monastery on a small mountain. Old trees and a resident hawk call this magical place home. With the soft breeze whistling through the majestic trees and the lone call of the hawk above me, how could I not quiet my mind from all the chaos and become present instead of worried about the future? It was so easy to close my eyes and just breathe the fresh air. I would listen to the world around me, relax, and become one with it.

You may enjoy trying different types of meditation.

There are many meditation styles; what matters is finding what works for you. Some, such as Transcendental Meditation (developed by Maharishi Mahesh Yogi and often called TM), use mantras. In Buddhism's Zen/Zazen meditation, you gain clarity by paying attention to your breath and your mind, and the teacher is an important guide.

If you like the feel of meditating with a group, you may like Mindfulness Based Stress Reduction classes. This type of meditation is well known and accepted by hospitals and psychologists. Mindfulness began with the teachings of Jon Kabat-Zinn.

The Labyrinth is another way to release your mind. It is a simple concept and yet it is very powerful.

A very good friend of mine and expert on labyrinths, Nancy Thiel Vogel, has honored us with her reasons labyrinths work so well with meditation:

Walk the path; your true voice awaits.

I delight in using my labyrinth as a meditation tool. I actively studied meditation four times a week with a guru for over a year and found that I needed to sit in meditation for at least twenty minutes before that blissful state of mindfulness would appear. What I discovered after having built a triple spiral labyrinth in my backyard was that I could arrive at that blissful state in the 2 ½ minutes it took to walk to the center of the labyrinth. I believe the speed is related to the inclusion of my body in the search/desire for mindfulness. I'll describe how I use mine and let you discover for yourself your "best practices" for using a labyrinth as a meditation tool.

I approach my labyrinth with excitement and knowledge that something magical is about to happen and that I never know exactly how it will show up or what that magic will look like. Standing at the entrance to the labyrinth, I pause to take in the beauty of the three connected spirals and take three slow, deep breaths, drinking in the sounds of nature around me, the feel of my bare feet on the ground (if it's warm enough to be barefoot), the scent of the trees and earth, the taste of fresh air. And then

I head in, following impulses as I go. This is where my way differs from traditional labyrinth walking. In my labyrinth, if my body wants to run or jump or skip or slither or crawl, then that is what I do. I don't usually talk, though I encourage sound. Laughter is welcome on my labyrinth, as is crying or growling or whimpering. Whatever is emerging is met and accepted and loved to the best of my ability (I sometimes find it hard to love my anger and my sadness and my fear, and then I turn my attention to loving the one in me who doesn't love my anger or sadness or fear.) I move through the spirals, marveling at the gyrations of my mind and noticing things like the tempo of my gait, the feel of the earth beneath my feet, the sound of the bird just above me. All these noticings bring me to the present moment. It's in the present moment that mindfulness can be found. I wind my way in to the center and I stand there, as I did at the entrance, and breathe, pausing until my body tells me it's time to move and then I wind back out.

So far, my explorations of the labyrinth as a meditation tool have brought me peace, answers that have surprised me, ideas and creative flow that have delighted me and directions that I never expected. One thing that I always find is that no matter what problem I enter with, it never seems as big as when I went in. I always leave with some level of clarity around the issue or I come away with a completely different question from the one I walked in with. My invitation is to find a labyrinth, either a walkable one on the ground or a picture of one to trace with your mind's eye, or one large enough to trace with your finger, and play. See what your impulses tell you. Follow the impulses that bring you delight and await the wonder!

For those who would like total relaxation and rejuvenation, Transcendental Meditation is said to increase the overall coherence of your brain waves. This working together of the brain waves continues through the day.

Twenty minutes two times a day in pure, relaxed bliss can help every part of your life. You silently repeat a mantra to enter into a state of profound calmness.

Mary Glasser is a certified teacher, director of Transcendental Meditation™. Licensed by the organization Global Country of World Peace. She describes how she discovered this type of meditation and its benefits.

A Teacher's Story

It began in my adolescent years: a vague sense that there had to be more. True happiness, a deeper connection with myself, a way to express the creative ideas I knew were inside, remained out of reach. My search led me to yoga, music, and various attempts at meditation, but still a kind of inner loneliness continued, and contentment eluded me.

It wasn't until a cold January day found me trudging through the snow to meet my TM teacher and receive my own personal mantra that my life began to truly take a new, more positive direction. I'd dabbled in various forms of meditation off and on, but they invariably left me frustrated or wanting. Inner peace seemed to be an unachievable goal for me. That all changed with my first TM meditation. I felt my body sink deeper into the chair as my mind drifted purposefully within as if on a journey to a new and as of yet, unknown destination. Before I knew what had happened, I found myself in a deep place of peaceful calm, unaware of any thoughts, yet fully awake inside.

As the days and weeks passed, my life quietly began to transform. All the anxiety which had been the final push to learn TM completely lifted. In its place I found a burgeoning joyfulness, as if rising up from deep within my being. Sleep became a totally new experience. Where before I'd tossed and turned for hours, waking more tired than before going to bed, I now found myself falling asleep within minutes and waking refreshed. Even though I was living the less than {ED: Word missing here?} lifestyle of a student, my health began to improve and I no longer worried about how I'd get through all the papers that needed to be written and the mountain of books to be read. It just seemed to happen, almost without effort. In addition, I rediscovered my love of music and found a new, creative outlet in art.

The transformation was so profound that my mother, a devout Catholic whom I had elected not to inform of my newfound meditation practice, began to inquire about what I was doing, and soon after, took to TM herself. Well into her mid-nineties today, she leads a very active independent life and takes almost no medications.

As the university semesters passed, I continued to meditate, while the looming question of "What do I want to do with my life?" remained unanswered. There seemed to be too many options. All I wanted was to find my true path in life. About two years into my TM practice, I realized there was no decision to make. I knew without doubt that my life's work would be around TM. A few more years and it was clear that I needed to bring this gift of self-knowledge to others, and I became a teacher. Now, thirty-two years later, I only wish that I could give everyone this gift which I now know is our birthright: the gift of effortless transcending, the gift of finding one's true Self, the key to true happiness.

Discover the inner you

Personalize your meditation for the best results.

I have found that experimenting with different forms of meditation can be fun. Soon you will find what works best for you. As with anything, there are many roads to the same destination. The goal is to use whatever works and helps you to discover the inner you. As you relax more often, you may find that your mind slows down and starts to dream. No, not sleep, but dream. Where do your dreams take you? Once you get the hang of relaxing and listening to everything around you, start to guide yourself with questions. Or ask for guidance for whatever answers you are looking for on that day. You can focus on your strengths or on healing the hurt or betrayal you may feel. Guided meditations can take you on a journey to find the answers or healing within you.

All of this takes time. The most important aspect of being in your place is to relax and become present and one with all around you. This is your place, your safe zone. Allow yourself to enjoy without pressure. This is only for you.

If you have trouble shutting out worry, doubt, and more, think of it as giving yourself a mini vacation. Sometimes we feel so validated in our worry or justified in our feeling wrong that we don't really want to stop thinking about it. So simply take a vacation. Allow your body and mind to feel what it is like to be free for just a short time. Then if you want to get back to the worry, that is your decision. But know that it is in this quiet place that the important answers lie. It is here where your strength, peace, compassion, and true confidence wait for you to discover them

As Deepak Chopra states it so clearly, meditating is not being quiet, but finding the quiet that is "already there – buried under 50,000 thoughts."

Amazingly, it is finding and relaxing into this quiet that helps us decipher our thoughts and put order back into our lives.

A Time to Explore

Achieving the quiet and calm along with becoming present, relaxing and discovering the inner you is the main reason to begin to meditate. When you feel ready, this is also a time to start exploring your life. As you begin, be sure to look at the events of your life from an objective viewpoint. You are observing and questioning. How did you end up where you are now? Why do you feel unfulfilled, unhappy? Can you identify what it is that is missing in your life? You can also search for the things that bring you joy. What are some of the places that bring you joy? What makes your heart just sing when you think of doing it? What is a passion you have always had and really never gave time to? Or, if you are not ready for these questions, you can stop all the thinking and become present and one with everything around you. This is your time, so you choose and go at your own speed.

This time is to help put you back in control of your destiny. It also helps with your perception of your situation and realization of what is truly important. Different days can bring up different questions or feelings. Some questions you can start with could be: What in your present situation is causing your dissatisfaction? What is your part in this situation? How do you perceive yourself? How do you want to perceive yourself? By accepting our situation and allowing ourselves to feel the sadness or hurt, without becoming overwhelmed, we can learn from it. What led up to the hurt and what was our part in it? Why do we find ourselves in our prison? What inside ourselves moved us to be where we are now? By asking and answering objectively, we can learn how to grow past it, to put it all into perspective.

Meditation became my safe zone. Once I felt myself relax, breathe deeply and connect to all the energy around me, I felt safe enough to look at my history, present, and future. I could see everything with a bird's eye view and feel unattached. That is because I felt connected to the world, the universe, and to my own divine inner self. If I was ever going to gain a clear picture of my life, this would be the time.

"You have to leave the city of your comfort zone, and go into the wilderness of your intuition. What you'll discover is yourself."
—ALAN ALDA

Meditation and getting to know yourself is the first step to discovery and healing. Putting everything into perspective and going forward with your life in a positive way is the benefit of meditation. You can't change the past but you can make a better future. Once you start to meditate every day, you will begin to look forward to this time as your time to be quiet and look over your questions or situation and look into yourself. Depending on what you are working on, the answers can be awesome or sometimes sad. But this helps us heal. It is an important step for you. You owe this to yourself and your future.

Start meditating for fifteen minutes. If you are comfortable meditating, great. If you are a people person, you might consider joining a meditation group. Sometimes this can help you relax. There is also a lot of friendship in a meditation group. It is up to you.

Take Time to Focus:

1. Pick a place that gives you peace and energy. If sitting is too difficult, try walking in a quiet park or in the woods or even an open field of flowers. Whether you are sitting or walking, begin to breathe deeply, allow your body to relax and your mind to float.

2. After your meditation, take the time to write down what you have discovered. If you did not work with any questions, then write what you heard or what it was like to be so calm, listening. How did it feel?

3. Start to explore your life: Write how you perceive yourself in the situation now. Write out how you would like to see yourself handle the situation in the future. What is the major difference?

4. What would you like your future to be? How would the future be different? How do you wish to proceed in the situation you are in currently?

5. Meditate each day. Every time will get easier and easier. You will discover more and more.

AFFIRMATION: I, _(insert name)_, am on a journey to discover me. In order to discover, heal, look to the future, and develop me, I will meditate every day and note whatever is discovered during meditation. I am excited to see my potential and the life that will bring me joy.

Date:_____

CHAPTER 7

Loving the Change:

Transitional Growth

*Once we understand that no matter how transition
comes into our life
what we decide concerning how we want to grow
and where we want to go,
we will begin to not fear transitions*

f one decides to research the word "transition", the word would be used to describe transitioning to the afterlife or from one job to another or from working to retirement. However people go through transitions all the time. I have come to think of transition as the end of one life cycle into another. Transitions happen from the time we are born into this world. We enter the non-physical to the physical. Our mind and senses absorb anything and everything. As we grow into children we are presented with the transition of home life to beginning school life. Entering into high school presents us with many transitions along with getting married or starting a career. Each advancement has a transition period. This is a time of personal growth. I think of it as growing into a new pair of shoes. Our feet are too big for the old shoes but just a little too small for the new. Transitions are the time we grow comfortably into our new shoes or new life cycle.

Sometimes transitions are difficult or unwanted such as going through a divorce or loss of a job. These harder transitions seem to come as a surprise – we aren't ready for them. We are suddenly thrown into a world we aren't sure about. Life seems cruel and unjust. When I and my now ex-husband decided that divorce was the only option, I was shocked. It felt as if I had fallen into the twilight zone. What was going to happen? How would we live? Could I support my children? Why was I alone again? All the feelings and uncertainty filled my head making it difficult to think or see my situation clearly. I just wanted time to stop and give me a chance to catch up. That is when I decided to take time to just drive and think. The feeling of moving but still having calmness inside the car seemed to help me breath. I was able to begin to absorb the shock and start to think about how to proceed. I mourned parts of my married life and began to see why the end of my marriage really was best for all. My car rides were a type of meditation, reflection and allowed me to have time to accept.

If you are dealing with a dramatic transition, it is only natural to mourn the loss. A marriage is definitely a very big loss. Men and women alike grieve the loss of their marriage, something they thought would last forever.

Grieving or mourning is a way of saying goodbye. You should allow it and really feel it. However, feel it for what it is, an end of that cycle of your life. Sometimes news of our partner wanting a divorce can come as a surprise, or we may not want to break up our marriage. Yes, this is difficult. You may want to mourn with blame and anger mixed in. It is important to begin to see the situation for what it is and accept without blame and anger. As the shock wears off, take time to grieve the good parts of the marriage. Although I was very unhappy for a quite a few years, I still mourned the separation of our family. Take time to say goodbye! Do what you need to do to get yourself to a place of acceptance. Once you gain this perspective you can begin to move forward.

There is one very important warning I would like to share with you: DO NOT shut yourself off from life to grieve. I realize you may just want to hide under the covers of your bed — but don't. Not only does this prolong the grief, it may also cause you to put yourself in victimhood. You blame yourself, your soon-to-be-ex and life itself. It is a pity party. The problem with it is that it is selfish. If you have a family, it is vital that you understand they are mourning also. Children are not immune to their families being dismantled. Thinking you are the only one suffering is a false belief. Your family, friends or anyone close to you is looking to you to make sure you and they will remain okay and strong. Grief is fine; self -pity does not bring good to anyone, including yourself.

Transitions can present us with forks in the road or choices. Once we accept our circumstance then we can look at the choices. Choices on where we want our lives to go. Choices of how we want to live our lives. Choices on how we want to feel. We all have forks in the road of our lives. Which road do we want to take? When we open our eyes clearly we see endless possibility. If we allow fear, doubt and worry, our eyes can only see limitation.

It is very possible to actually bloom through our transition and into our new life cycle. That is where we are heading anyway. Wouldn't it be to our betterment to make the absolute best new life cycle as possible? Why would we want to transition into the same problem or worse? But in order for us to have positive growth into an amazing life we first need to accept where we are in the present and where we want to go for the future? And finally, begin a plan to get started? Who do we want to become? All these questions are necessary to give us a sense of perspective, control and purpose. Also it helps us to deal with all the changing of our daily routines and the meaning behind them.

When you are going through a transition in your life, no matter how small, you change habits. A friend once mentioned that habits were what people mourned the most. It is the disruption in our lives, the sudden feeling of chaos. How many habits you change depends on how big the transition.

The shock of divorce can cause a person to feel empty and totally uncertain. Everything seems surreal, almost like you are floating. Focusing on daily tasks, let alone knowing where you are going, seems impossible.

Not only was I losing my spouse, but my whole daily life was changed. The routines, like making a family dinner, putting the children to bed together, and sleeping with someone, were all disrupted. It was up to me to carry on doing all the tasks myself. Everything I had known as a spouse had changed. Of course I grieved these changes.

These routines or habits we perform every day to make our daily life smoother may seem small, but they're not. Now these same habits can become a constant reminder of what is not anymore, creating an atmosphere of even more uncertainty.

Scientific studies have shown how changing one habit can cause us to feel uncertain or uneasy. I decided to try my own experiment. I asked my family to try to do everything with their non-dominant hand. That meant that cutting, eating, writing, drinking from a glass, absolutely everything must be done with the hand we never really use. This experiment was to last for three days. Because all of us were participating we had a lot of fun with the experiment, however it was very difficult. Every part of our day took longer. We constantly had to stop ourselves from using our dominant hand. All of the easy daily tasks now became difficult and sloppy. If my family and I had a problem just because we consciously decided to change what hand to use, then it stands to reason that when you are forced to change many daily habits you really do not want to change, you can feel like your world has gone upside down.

I find that if the transition is for something I really want, the habit changes happen easily. Likewise, if a transition is needed or forced like with a death, uncertain job change, or move, the habits can be harder to change. Sometimes habits can be hard to change because something is blocking us. This is usually because of a paradigm or old belief that doesn't want the change. We will discuss paradigms later.

It is important to realize and accept that our daily habits need to change as we transition and grow. "It is what it is." Take a deep breath and accept. If you are changing many daily habits, make a schedule that you like. You can even have a little fun with it.

Write a list of what now needs to be accomplished on a daily basis. Start with your morning and list everything until bedtime. Be sure to include even the littlest daily task. Next, give a task a time, making sure you allot the time the task needs. Now for the fun part: Make sure each day you have scheduled time for yourself. This time is for you to unwind, work on yourself, or treat yourself, and it is all yours. This is important for two reasons. First, it will take the weight off of having to change your schedule. Second, with all the changes, you need time to gather your thoughts and center yourself. As you read more in this book, you will see why it is so important.

By making a list, not only are you preparing for this new schedule and creating new habits, but you are allowing your mind to become used to the change. This next step will help you move through the transition with more ease. Read through the new schedule at least three to four times a day. Imagine yourself moving through the schedule easily and enjoying it. Have fun with it, knowing that your special time for you is coming every day. As you do this exercise, the new schedule will start to sink into your subconscious. Once the schedule is accepted by your mind, the feelings of uncertainty will diminish. You may still feel bits of sorrow from time to time, but this will also diminish as the new schedule becomes the norm.

As the schedule and the meditations start to become more routine, your situation is already starting to change. Take a look at the fork in the road and look inside you. Have you started on the path you really want? The answer lies inside you. Which road do you want your life to take? How do you want to handle your situation? Who do you really want to be as a person? And how do you want to feel when your transition is done? All these answers lie within you. It is time to find out. It is the beginning of a new cycle in your life!

Once I accepted where I was in my life and began to move forward in my thoughts and actions, I saw with clearer vision the path I wanted to proceed. Conquering the changing of my habits and getting used to being alone started to get easier. I wanted with all my heart to be strong and make good decisions for myself and my family.

You will see more than two options. There may be five or six ideas come to you. That is fine. The important point is that you are creating your future. As I stated before, you will know what your life is to be. Who do you want to be? How do you want to handle your life and this transition? Yes, these are all choices, and the answers are inside you. It is time to calm yourself and listen. It is your life, not your mom's, father's, brother's, sister's, aunt's or uncle's, and certainly not your soon-to- be-ex's life. It is yours! If you do not know what you want or who you really are, others will be glad to define it for you. But it is your life only. You are the creator of your future. What do you want?

Tom had his life turn upside down. He learned his wife wanted a divorce in the same week he learned that he was being transferred to a position in another state. Everything was changing, but Tom had not asked for any change. Sometimes life just decides you need to grow, whether you like it or not. Tom accepted the job transfer and promotion, then immediately started to mourn the loss of his former life. He didn't really know what he was supposed to do. Everything he had known for seventeen years was gone. I would not be surprised if there were days he wanted to just hide under the covers, but he did not hide. In fact, he started to meditate and made up his new schedule. He wanted clarity on how to deal with this huge transition. He wanted to learn more about who he was and who he wanted to be. He loved his job and was sure the promotion was right for him. But what about the move and the divorce? The two answers he was certain of were, he wanted to move forward into his new life in a positive way and he wanted the decisions concerning the divorce to be in the best interest of the whole family.

He decided to visit the city he would soon be living in for his new job. He also met with some of the people at his new job. He liked the people, the climate, and even found a nice condo. His career life was looking pretty good and Tom found himself becoming a little excited.

As he continued to meditate and visualize the type of person he wanted to be during his divorce, he was able to see what was in the best interest of the children. So he asked his lawyer to request a mediation. Whenever he spoke with his soon-to-be-ex, he would bring up how he hoped they could work together for the best interest of the children. When they had their mediation they were able to settle everything, because both parties were on the same page and working together.

Tom had accepted the situation he found himself in. He was at a place in his life where he could have easily given up and become depressed. Instead, he organized himself and discovered more about himself. He looked inside himself for the answers on how to proceed with his life. As the answers became clearer, he understood more about how to make the necessary changes in his thoughts and actions to create less stress during the divorce and his new life. He was starting to think more in terms of what would benefit the family instead of reacting with anger, revenge, and frustration.

Tom understood that by taking responsibility for how he wanted to handle his transition and focusing on what he wanted the result to be, how he wanted to present himself and what was in the best interest for all, he created a better world for himself and those around him.

How will you handle your transition? What are some of the results you want to see?

Once we understand that no matter how transition comes into our life what we decide concerning how we want to grow and where we want to go, we will begin to not fear transitions. We will not hold on to a life that has passed us by. We won't live with bitterness or anger over the past. That cycle of our life is gone. It will never return. I could not bring back the good part of my marriage. It was gone. My marriage was gone. What lays before me is change. What type of change do I want to have? Where do I want it to lead? With these questions I can take control of my future life – I can take control of who I want to be.

From the very start, Tom moved towards his future and he was excited. Yes, he did grieve, but it is not only a time to say goodbye. For him, it is also a time to say hello to his life. For our family, it was evolving into our new life cycle. We have grown closer and gained more compassion for each other. Although the ending of the life cycles were different, the process of creating our new life cycle is very much the same. Changing our habits and becoming who we want to become. It is only a desire away! What is yours?

No matter what you may see as your present situation, allow yourself to imagine who you want to grow to be? What is in your heart to do? Once you begin to set your mind on these questions with faith that anything is possible – thy will be done. My client Louise had not one cent to her name. Lawyers did not want to take her divorce case. However, Louise did not give up. She saw in her mind a home for her children and a job as an interior decorator. She believed with her whole heart and acted like it would not be any other way. With pure will and faith Louise pursued her desire and achieved her goal. Her children have a nice, warm house to call home, she has her dream job as an interior decorator and she finally has a lawyer who is guiding her through the divorce process.

Yes, it does take time to grieve, get over the shock and then, start to accept. That is the true starting point. Once you accept with an open mind and bring forth what is in your heart – the sky is the limit.

Do you know what you want to be? What type of person? And what is in your heart? What is your purpose? Not sure?

Then it is time to come with me and let's discover you!

Take Time to Focus:

1. Take time to grieve. Find your perfect place to reflect and accept. It may be a car, nature moving to music, whatever helps you process is great. Just do it! You will not regret the time you take to heal.

2. Write out: 1) Whom do you want to be during this transition? How do you want to feel and be perceived by others? 2) What do you want to do in the new life cycle coming after the transition? What are you getting ready or growing into being?

3. Write out your new schedule. Even if you want only to lose a little weight, write out your eating schedule. Read through it at least twice a day until it is the new norm. You are helping your mind adjust easily.

4. During your meditations, ask for clarity on the situation you are leaving behind. Look at it objectively. How do you want to handle leaving? What would be in the best interest of all involved? Even if you are not leaving, but changing your situation, how can it change and benefit all involved? Write out the results you want to see. Write out how your thoughts and actions can help you achieve your desired results.

AFFIRMATION: I, _(*insert name*), understand that I can deal with my transitions by moving forward in a positive way without causing harm to anyone. It is my time to grow and I choose to grow in the best way I can as a person. I will take responsibility for my actions and words to achieve positive results.

Date_____.

CHAPTER 8

What a Truly Wonderful World!:

Gratitude

It all starts with feeling grateful
As that feeling grows and you receive more and
more to be grateful for, you begin to enter
the world of complete wonder.

Not feeling grateful was my wake-up call as I sat in my car feeling the warmth of the sun. Feeling grateful was a virtue my parents encouraged. When I found that I could not say thank you to Infinite Source or the Universe I realized that life had to change.

Many psychologists, counselors and even teachers are telling people dealing with depression, anxiety or just too much stress to wake up in the morning and, first thing, make a list of what they are thankful for in their lives. This small step has been shown to greatly benefit a person's outlook on life. Even if you are not struggling with depression or anxiety, living in your own prison is a stressful time. Being grateful is a blessing for everyone, no matter what we are going through.

The act of being grateful not only helps us to see beauty and how fortunate we are. It shows us that there are aspects of our life that are good. If we really feel or internalize the feeling of gratefulness or the goodness of our life, it will help us to raise our vibration, move forward in our life from a happier point and allow us to see with a clearer perspective.

Everyone has something to be grateful for in life. Sometimes, when we concentrate on only the negative, we don't even recognize the blessings. I was very unhappy and lost in my marriage. Even though I loved my children, I did not feel the gratitude or how truly blessed I was because I only allowed myself to see how hard every day was with my spouse. Once I began to open my eyes to the miracle of my beautiful children and feel the love from and for them, my world started to change.

Why does gratefulness work? What is it about gratefulness that allows our lives to improve almost immediately? It has to do with two key concepts. Realization that your life is not as bad as you have led yourself to believe and these blessings, no matter how small, are gifts to be treasured. There is always something to be grateful for in our lives – children, parents, what you may feel is a lucky break, the roof over your head or the food you eat are all blessings. When we understand and feel grateful for the blessings in our life, we move forward happier, seeing more things that bring us gratefulness or happiness. As the gratitude for my family grew, I started to see beauty everywhere. While driving I would notice the uniqueness of the sky each morning. People who greeted me with smiles or the gift of an unexpected conversation. The happier I became the more opportunities appeared to bring other blessings. This leads me to the

FEELING CHART IN WAVES

Alena Chapman

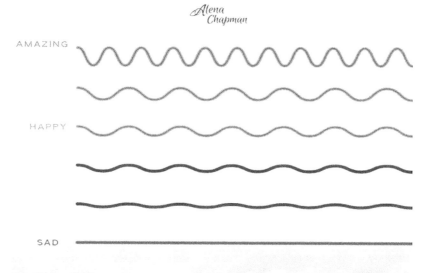

AMAZING

HAPPY

SAD

second concept, which is vibration. As I became happier, I was actually raising my vibration.

Vibration is a popular buzz word in many circles; however, few people really understand how vibration works in their lives. The Law of Vibration is one of the primary Universal Laws. Meaning, it is one of the laws that our whole universe operates under. Other primary laws of the Universe are the Law of Cause and Effect, the Law of Polarity, which is the law of opposites and the Law of Gestation, which is the law of time to mature, such as a seed germinating into a plant. The Law of Vibration states that everything is energy and functions at a certain frequency. The table or chair is energy; the trees and plants are energy; you and I are energy; the air we breathe and the water we drink breaks down into energy. Everything is energy. The table vibrates at a slower/different frequency than water. The tree vibrates at a different frequency than a person.

What does this Law of Vibration have to do with being grateful? It seems that scientists are now studying thought as a frequency. They already seem to agree that thought travels and are starting to measure how fast and how far it travels. This means that a sad thought vibrates at one frequency and a happy thought vibrates at another frequency. It has been shown that a happy thought travels faster and farther than a sad thought.

If happy thoughts are on a certain vibration and sad thoughts are on another vibration, that means when we think a happy thought we are on the happy frequency and if we think a sad thought, we are on the sad frequency.

Now, here is the importance of this information. If our thoughts are on one frequency, we will receive more of that frequency in our life. This means that if I have sad thoughts, I am on a sad frequency and will receive more sadness in my life to feed my thought process. It is like turning on a country music station on the radio. What will you hear? Country music. And if you turn on a classical station you will hear classical music. You will not hear country music on the classical station, nor will you hear classical music on the country station. This is exactly how the frequency of our thoughts works.

As my eyes opened to the beauty and opportunities to be grateful in my life, I became happy and even filled with wonder. The beauty of the moonlight on the water or the fun I had sledding down the hill with my children would raise my vibration to amazement. History has found that Einstein would have his chauffeur drive him every morning out to a field. He would then get out of the car carrying a violin. First, he would stand in the field listening to the birds and looking at the sunrise. Then he would begin to play the violin as tears of overwhelming gratefulness for the beauty filled him.

It all starts with feeling grateful. As that feeling grows and you receive more and more to be grateful for, you begin to enter the world of complete wonder. This is where I personally think the magic of life begins. This is the frequency of creativity and unlimited possibilities. All we need to do is start with being grateful and allow it to change our perception.

How to begin

List five things you are grateful for every morning when you get up and before you go to bed. After you make your list, read it over a few times. As you read allow your mind to really consider why you are grateful. For instance, if I am thankful for my children, I would think of what a wonderful blessing they are, how they bring joy to my life, maybe even an event or experience which shows the happiness and joy they have brought to my life. Read your grateful list out loud, raising it up to God, or the universe. The idea is to have feeling or emotion as you read. Just reading your list will do nothing. You must have emotion in order to internalize the thankfulness. By internalizing it, you are starting to create a thankful heart.

With this thankfulness, you too will begin to see the beauty around you. It could be how the moonlight dances on the water or the wind creates music as it blows through the trees. Becoming grateful for these special gifts puts the world, our world, into perspective. You will find, if you allow it, you will begin to enjoy feeling this happiness. That is when you begin to notice little things during your day that bring even more gratitude and happiness. Soon you feel happiness even when circumstances may be difficult.

Divorce can become very "me" oriented, especially if we allow ourselves to be put in the role of a victim. But any time we feel that life is doing things to us, we become a victim. "Look what is happening to me." "Look what they are doing to me." With all the "me" being abused, there is no room for anything else. Often, there isn't really any room for our families. It is always about "me." Now that you understand about frequency and vibration, you can see how being a victim is its own vibration. It is a vibration of insecurity, and sympathy. It constantly needs reassurance and is centered entirely on staying a victim. So of course the only thing you see are things that make you more of a victim. You can't be thankful if you are always feeling you are a victim or you are living in a world of revenge. How very sad because so much is passing you by.

But when you are grateful, you see the strength God has given you. Strength to get through any difficult situation. Strength to move into your life. You will see strength as a blessing and give thanks. You will appreciate all the gifts given to us every day through nature, friends, and family. You will feel fortunate and realize how truly blessed you are. You will see what is truly important in your life and what is not important. What is the overall picture in your situation? What truly is a gift and benefits everyone in the family? What is the overall picture of your life? Seeing the overall picture will help you get through without getting dragged down into the muck of it. It also allows you to see exactly what is going on with your children and family. You can see more clearly because you are looking with a grateful heart.

Once I raised my vibration through gratefulness I was able to see the many blessings I received every day through the angels put in my path to help me and my children through difficult times. I felt the confidence of my perception and my ability to not panic or worry, but instead see what needed to be done and what was real and what was only smoke. I am still filled with gratitude for all the blessings from people and events that helped me grow and keep my family strong throughout turmoil. Angels were the awesome friends and family who stayed by me, guiding and supporting me. Angels taught me to forgive and let go. Angels worked with me to watch over my children in school and help them adjust to our new lives. I really feel that it was an infinite force that brought me to a lawyer who understood me and helped me so much. This Infinite Source/God/the Universe also provided me with opportunity to help others get through their divorces with more confidence, purpose and compassion. It is with a grateful heart that I saw these angels and opportunities that helped me grow and led to where I am today.

So often clients will come to me complaining, seeing only the bad in their lives. But once they open their eyes to the gratitude, they begin to move forward in their lives because they can see the possibilities and begin to believe in themselves.

There is an old story about a man and a flood. The water filled the town. One man ran to his roof and prayed on his knees, "God, please save me from this flood." Soon a person on a raft floated by.

"Hey, sir, come on. I have room," the person yelled.

"No, I am waiting for God to save me," replied the man on the roof. The raft floated on down the street.

After a little while a canoe paddled up to the man's roof. "Hop in," said the person in the canoe.

"No, thank you; my God is going to save me," said the man on the roof. The canoe paddled on.

Finally a motor boat came up to the roof. "Sir, the flood is getting worse. Let me take you to safety," urged the man in the motor boat.

"You don't understand. I trust that my God will save me. I am in good hands," the man on the roof righteously replied.

I love this story. The man on the roof was focused only on his problem and his need. He did not thank God for having a roof above the flooding waters where he could rest until help could come to him. He was not grateful for all the boats coming to save him. He didn't even see that God was sending him the boats to save him.

You have boats arriving every day in your life. The Universe is waiting for you to open your eyes and start to receive its gifts. Now is the time to jump on a boat or a better frequency. Say "thank you" for the gifts no matter how small. Then and only then will you begin to see the opportunities and angels that are waiting to help you move into your future.

To this day, I always write and read my grateful list before I start my day and again before I meditate. If I am not in nature, but in my home, I light candles, play some meditative music and write and read my list.

Being grateful puts you in a higher vibration. It helps you to see better when you meditate.

Now I cannot imagine driving the kids to school and not noticing the sunrise or the deer that might cross our path. I can't imagine not noticing the good people I meet every day or the events of the day when they go smoothly. I cannot imagine being so lost in myself that I am not thankful for the gifts I receive every single day.

Start today and get your list together. Read it, internalize it, and offer it up to the universe or God. How do you feel? Every day will get easier. Also, as you drive or walk down the road, name two or three things that brings you a feeling of immense gratitude or joy.

What a truly wonderful world we live in! How blessed we are every day by gifts entering our lives. Opportunities surround us every moment. At every moment we receive a new chance to start anew. What a truly wonderful life we live.

Think of three things you see or experience that you are grateful for. You might even find yourself being thankful all day. It is a wonderful world and it is time to start noticing it.

Take Time to Focus:

If having a grateful heart was the only lesson you chose to learn, you would still grow as a person. If you truly apply being grateful with everything in your life, you will be amazed at the results you will see.

1. Find some time to take a walk in a beautiful park or anywhere you can see the glory of nature. Notice the peace, the animals, the breeze, and the sound it makes as it blows through the leaves of the trees. Take a breath in, let it out slowly, and relax. Give thanks.

2. Have a pad of paper or notebook just for giving thanks. On the top of the page write, "I am so happy and grateful that:" . . . First thing in the morning, write what you are thankful for that will

happen during the day. Allow yourself to feel the happiness. For instance, if I am going to teach a class today, I am happy and grateful for all the students, for being able to touch their lives in a positive way, for everything I may learn and for helping the students reach their goals. Now read through your list and feel the joy and potential for the day.

3. At night, list five more things you are grateful for. This time list things that have happened or that you have. You could be happy and grateful for all the wonderful people you met today, finishing an important project, making a decision to change your life, or your children or family. After you have made your list, read it through and allow yourself to feel the happiness.

4. During the day, take notice of your surroundings. Look at the marvels we have in our world. The more you open your eyes, the more you will see. Notice the people that help or are happy or opportunities that may occur. Give thanks and again allow yourself to feel the happiness.

You will start to be grateful automatically. When this happens, you will feel your mood lift and you will feel good. When you feel good. What a Truly Wonderful World We Live In!

AFFIRMATION: I, *(insert name_)*, will consciously work to open myself up to our glorious world and its many gifts by daily giving thanks. I do this so that I may gain a grateful heart and see the joy, love, beauty, and opportunities that abound. I will do this in order that I may always be grateful and happy. I am so happy and grateful for my life.

Date:_____

CHAPTER 9

Incredibly Worthy of It All:

Value of Self

So often we punish ourselves instead of thanking ourselves.
Why?
As you are becoming more grateful
for this wonderful world, be grateful for you.

What does it mean to value oneself? To many this doesn't even enter their minds. However, to value oneself is one of the most important aspects of growth. It is valuing yourself that allowed you to pick up this book and want to break out of your prison.

Many self-help gurus and psychologists say that we cannot give what we do not have. If we do not have the love and respect for ourselves how would we know how to give it to others? How do we teach it to our children? To feel the inner strength, confidence in our choices, compassion for all around you and most of all allow your light to shine, you must accept and value the divine in you.

We all have energy that connects us to everyone and the universe. Knowing this, why would we put ourselves down or feel that we do not deserve to treat ourselves well? Why do we not have the confidence to stand for what we know is right for us? Why do we allow others to control, bully or criticize our ideas and dreams?

The feeling of being whole or complete really does encompass mind, body and soul. Our bodies are miraculous. They are what keep us on this physical plane so that we can live the experiences that evolve our mind and spirit. Our conscious mind thinks analytically, reasons and learns what we need to know in order to grow. This part of our mind also censors any information it feels is not important or untrue. Our subconscious mind has the gifts of spirit. The six gifts: imagination, intuition, will, perception, reason and memory all help us to see the truth and discover our purpose and possibilities. Every part of us has a reason or purpose. Each part of our mind, body and spirit work together to create who we are and our purpose. Honoring and growing every part of us is definitely honoring the universe and the gifts it has given us.

Now that you are beginning to discover your own beauty with meditation, acceptance and surrender, you are gaining more and more discovery and connection with the guidance inside you. This is you! When we take care of ourselves, treat ourselves with love, we are respecting the energy/soul and connection our Creator has given us. You will be amazed as judgment and harsh feelings fade and instead compassion and love will fill your heart.

Taking time to meditate, be grateful and look for the beauty of our world are all ways to begin valuing the divine in us. I have found with clients sometimes even with all of the wonder for the world and universe around them, they still do not feel they deserve to value themselves. Without valuing themselves they never begin to trust themselves. Without honoring who they are, others have influence over their decisions and actions. Boundaries are broken and dreams get held back.

Every day I will do something just for me. It doesn't have to be something big or take a lot of time. It just has to be for me. For me it helps me gain perspective when the day may not be going the way I have planned. One example would be of an extremely busy Saturday. Saturdays are always busy but this particular Saturday was the worst. I had the typical weekend, driving kids to all their activities; however, this Saturday there seemed to be much more. At one point my oldest got into the car and said, "I have two other rehearsals I need to get to." I felt frustration that I would never be able to get out of the car again. Instead of letting this bad mood grow I announced that we were going to stop at a coffee shop. Once there I got out of the car to go in and order a tea. My child reminded me that we did not really have time for this and I responded we were making the time. Once inside I talked with people, listened to the music as I waited for my order. I took a deep breath and relaxed. Once I got back into the car I announced we would listen to my music. I was content again. That little break I gave myself was enough to change my mood and give me perspective. I began to plan how I could get some work done as I waited in the car for one or another of my children to finish a lesson or rehearsal. Even my son said, "Wow, you seem much happier." The best part is that my children benefit from my happiness.

Many people place other people's needs above their own. This can cause them to feel put upon and unappreciated, it is really the lack of value they give themselves — not meeting their own needs or desires — that causes them to feel this way. If we respect and value ourselves and our time, then we respect and value others and their time.

Taking time out of each day is not difficult and has much benefit for you. It doesn't have to take a lot of time or be expensive. Maybe it is taking time to walk with the dog, stopping to get your favorite tea or coffee, reading a book you have always wanted to read or whatever that something for you may be. Just a little something special for you.

If my day is going to be long and stressful, doing something a little special will help ease the "yuk" feeling. Divorce can have days when you want to say "yuk" a lot. Sometimes the stress can be overwhelming. Just taking a drive or walking in the park and breathing deep breaths can relax you.

I remember finding my little mountain. It had been a very stressful day with normal divorce issues and on top of that, there were the attacks from whomever was attacking me, my children and our home. I went for a drive and after following a stone fence up this mountain, I found an old monastery with very old trees and a majestic hawk. I would sit on the mountain overlooking the town below and watch my hawk fly above me. I was so immensely grateful for the peace, reassurance and supportive energy I received. This became my sacred space. I remember thanking myself for taking the time to find this magnificent place. Consciously find your special moments and treasure them. Then feel grateful.

However, so often we punish ourselves instead of thanking ourselves. Why? As you are becoming more grateful for this wonderful world, be grateful for you. You are a product of this world, God and the universe. We are part of the glory. Once we realize this, it changes who we are and the world around us.

"Setting aside to take care of yourself is not being selfish.
It is honoring yourself."
NYAMBURA MWANG

A popular concept of our time is to push ourselves through the situations or circumstances without a care for how it will affect us. Even when we are sick, we are supposed to keep going full steam ahead. We become tired, bitter and hard on ourselves. Why do we want to be and live this way? It isn't good for us mentally, emotionally or physically. It hurts those around us. Our family and friends feel our unhappiness and stress. If we feel unhappy, stressed, bitter or down on ourselves we will portray these very same feelings to everyone around us. Instead of just bulldozing our way through, stop and think what is the best for all in this situation. If I am sick, is it better for me to rest, not spread my germs and get everyone sick and heal and honor myself with rest? If it is an obstacle or challenge moving through with the use of our subconscious, trusting our inner voice and doing what is best for everyone involved led us to a life where we love ourselves and those around us even more. In fact, we love life more.

It is so important to practice gratitude and raise your vibration to one of opportunities and possibilities. Value you, your strength and your fortitude. Take the time to relax, enjoy time with yourself, be kind and gain new perspective on your life. Valuing yourself and your time is not only for hard circumstances. Allowing yourself to take time for you and enjoy tunes you into your body, mind, and spirit even more. When we value something, we listen to it more intently. So next time you hear yourself say, "I need some time just for me," you will take the time.

If I had chosen to bulldoze my way through a four and a half-year divorce, I would not have grown or bloomed. Instead, I would have been bitter, angry and unable to let go of my struggle. If I had allowed the stress of the people tormenting me grow into fear, I would not have been able to keep the right perspective of my situation. My world and my children's world would be very different and much harder if I did not practice the gratitude, value myself and transcend to a place where I could see the issues before me with a bird's-eye view. Because I valued myself and took the time to reenergize every day, I was able to see how to proceed for the best of all involved. Because I treated myself with respect and kindness, I also gave this respect and kindness to those around me, including my children.

Because of the value I gave myself, I was able to also give to my family!

I would put little treats in my children's backpacks about once a week to surprise them. I would include a little note to encourage them through the day or just say I was proud of them and loved them. When you are not happy, or going through a hard time, your kids bear the stress too. They may not say anything, but they know and feel everything. During my divorce I could see that my children were feeling stress. And why not; their family was being torn apart. The more I could be there for them and help them feel secure, that they are not alone, the better they would cope. I remember how the kids would get into the car after school excited and ask how I was able to get the snack into their bags without them knowing. Or how did I know they were nervous about the test they had to take that day? I always replied, "Moms have their way." Well, look at that, another thankful moment.

If we are what we think about or if our lives become what we think about, wouldn't it be better to be a person filled with wisdom, happiness and love and our lives filled with happiness, abundance and love? If we respect ourselves, listen to ourselves and follow our own guidance, wouldn't it stand to reason we would give more respect to those around us, listen clearer to what they have to say and help others to trust their own guidance? The only way we can give others our best is to treat ourselves well and be grateful for ourselves. Then giving our best is easy because we feel our best.

Taking the time to treat yourself special or recharge is a way to say, "Thank you, Divine Source, for creating me, giving me this experience. Thank you for me!" When you are able to freely say thank you in this way, you will never again feel that you do not deserve to live a life full of happiness and abundance. Never again will you question yourself or doubt yourself.

You deserve to be and do what you know deep inside is your purpose. You deserve the best life has to offer – to live the experience of life to its fullest. You deserve to treat yourself well and to be treated well, just as much as you treat others with respect, love and compassion. It all begins with you.

Take Time to Focus:

1. Think about something or someplace you have for your special "me time." What or where helps you to center and feel grateful and happy? Make sure you have easy access when you need it.

2. Now start to have your "me time" and be grateful for it. Do not let worries or frustrations enter. This is a time to recharge and be happy with you! You deserve this time very much.

3. As you are starting to make changes in yourself and your life, don't forget the people close to you. I talked about children, but you may have other people who have been affected by your unhappiness. Show them kindness and allow them in. They will feel special and included. They will also feel you are not trying to exclude them.

AFFIRMATION: I, _(*insert name*)__, am going to treat myself like the glorious creation of God/the universe. No more will I punish myself; instead, I know I am growing and am thankful for me and my life. I will take the time to recharge myself and treat myself well. I will internalize this feeling and pass it along to the people close to me and my children.

Date: _____

At this point, stop. Really, stop! Focus on your quiet meditations and your gratefulness. Read through the chapters again. My mentors would tell me to read a chapter for 30 days to really learn and absorb the teachings. Allow for special moments for you and your children. It takes time to relax and start getting answers or feeling the wholeness of everything. If you aren't used to doing any of these things, or the prison you are in is especially hard, it can take more time. So allow it to take more time. Just keep doing it. Keep finding that quiet space and if nothing else, relax or try being thankful for one thing in the morning and one thing in the afternoon or at bed- time. The key is to relax and allow everything to fall into place. The answers will come. Just allow yourself to relax and be thankful. You are the only one who can let yourself feel peace and joy.

Move forward with this book when you are ready. There is no hurry!

BOOK THREE
Focus

Yesterday is but a dream,
tomorrow is but a vision.
But today well lived makes
every yesterday
a dream of happiness,
and every tomorrow a vision of hope.
Look well, therefore,
to This Day.

CHAPTER 10

Lighten Your Load:

Forgiveness

*Forgiveness is about empowering yourself
rather than empowering your past.*

Now that you are taking responsibility for you, finding your connection to the Universe, and being grateful for where you are and the possibilities of where you are going, you are now beginning to grow. You are trusting the inner you and choosing how you respond and live your life. There is a new understanding and wisdom. With this wisdom comes compassion for yourself and all those around you — even those who may have caused you pain.

The time has come to start the process of forgiveness. Forgiveness can only be true if you are ready to forgive. Otherwise it is a useless exercise. Just as we have taken responsibility for our present and future, we must also take responsibility for our past. Our understanding of the connection and Divine Source provides us the clarity to know we must surrender any negative feelings that are holding us back. There is no reason to harbor punishment for ourselves or for others.

Forgiveness is about empowering yourself rather than empowering your past.

It is so easy to say we forgive, but how does your inner self react when you think of the person or situation that bothers you? Do you feel a tightening in your gut? Does your head begin to ache a little? Do your shoulders tighten? This is the attachment you still have — a ball and chain.

Hate and revenge and anger feel invigorating. People are eager to feed anger because they become invigorated also. However, you cannot move freely forward in your life if you are feeding what is in your past. The negative emotions will follow you into every aspect of your future. True freedom cannot be attained without forgiveness.

During the very beginning of my divorce, I felt anger, hurt, and confusion. So many friends and family members were willing to add to these feelings: "Well, what if your soon-to-be-ex does this? It is very possible that this or that will happen." Of course this or that was always bad. This would cause the anger to grow. The conversation would become very animated and alive. Why? Because anger and hurt are types of energy, very strong energy!

Negative emotions like anger and revenge can make a person feel totally alive. It is exhilarating, but this type of energy eats at the person who uses it. It will reside in your muscles, your thoughts, your actions, your digestive system, and your heart. People who continue to feed this type of energy and stress start to suffer in one way or another in their future relationships, their health, and the decisions they make for their lives.

More important is that this angry, vengeful person wants to hold on to the anger. They do not want to move forward because their focus is on how to feed the fire inside them. Their minds cannot see the positive and they cannot move on past the anger.

Letting go of these feelings of anger, hurt, and revenge releases the tension; the heaviness. Forgiveness opens our minds and hearts to positive feelings. Forgiveness allows us to move forward without baggage, accept things as they are, do things better, and create better relationships now and in the future.

Nothing you can do can change the past. So, why do we beat ourselves up over things that have happened? Why do we want to keep beating up others for things they have done in the past? Sometimes we don't even see them trying to be better because we can't let go of the past or the mistakes made. When we forgive ourselves for things we have done, it lifts a huge weight. Especially when we feel we have made a huge mistake. It is a feeling of starting over, doing everything better. We stop trying to beat ourselves up and instead take an objective look at why we made those mistakes and learn from them. Our whole life is a learning experience, so we are bound to make mistakes and learn. The purpose is to learn. Likewise, forgiving others allows us to let go of the hurt, anger and revenge. It allows us to see them trying to do better if they so choose. Once I took an objective look at my soon-to-be-ex, and where he was coming from or what in his past might have led to his mistake, I was able to forgive. What good is it to carry that weight? How can you move ahead with that anger inside? You really can't, especially in new relationships. You end up measuring everyone against that mistake. If you understand the mistakes for what they are and learn from them, you can let them go.

I remember hearing a judge say, "People can be very cruel to each other during a divorce." And this is very true. The person you gave your life to, had faith in and felt you knew inside and out is gone. Now there is a person who is angry, selfish and hurtful. When you can look on the situation with some objectivity and really see how one event caused another, you begin to understand how everything digressed to this point. You also begin to see the situation for what it was or is, you don't get pulled down in the mess, but instead keep focused on what is important for you and your family.

Evelyn was divorcing a very rich, successful man. Together they had four children, two of whom were adopted. Her soon-to-be-ex was the type of person who liked to win no matter what the cost or who it hurt. Evelyn was attacked personally, financially, and physically. Even the family dog was mysteriously poisoned. As Evelyn became more and more afraid, her sense of paranoia increased. To make matters worse her children, watching her fall apart, decided it was better to be with Daddy.

Absorbed in her victimhood, she gave up everything including her children in order to end the attacks she felt were because of the divorce. As soon as she signed the papers, her whole being felt empty. She had nothing left.

Evelyn came to me a few months after her divorce. She could not stop punishing herself for giving up her family, but she knew she had to start healing the hurt and anger. To start this healing process, she began to pray a prayer of healing, to meditate bringing light of healing and hope. As she worked through the tools of gratefulness, responsibility, and surrender, she began to understand and draw upon the strength she was beginning to find within herself.

Evelyn knew she had to forgive herself and her ex-husband if she was to gain the trust and love of her children again. She now understood her part in co-creating the problems that led to the divorce and the loss of her family. Her awareness revealed how her feelings of fear and victimhood prevented her from reaching out to provide the much-needed love and support. Instead, in her panic she had tried to control the family, causing separation and distrust.

Forgiveness took time and determination. Evelyn began by remembering the happy times with her now ex-husband. She saw his qualities that caused her to fall so deeply in love. Taking the good feelings, she began to see the events that led to the distance in her marriage. Slowly she gained objectivity and compassion. This enabled her to be able to see how and why each of them had acted the way they did throughout the end of the marriage and the divorce.

Evelyn also understood her ex-husband could provide for the children much better than she could at the present time. This was a hard realization, but it was a starting point. Forgiveness was providing vision for her future. She now knew she could rebuild her relationship with her children and act on her dreams to create her life.

The relationship between Evelyn and her children grew closer and more precious. She opened her heart to their questions and needs and in turn received all the love they had for her. Even though the children remained living with their father, she did not miss out on experiencing their growing years.

Forgiveness helps us let go of guilt, vengeance, feelings of inadequacy and pain. True loving forgiveness helps us to rise above our egos and blame. It helps us to start over with our lives and ourselves. It also removes our attachment and gets rid of the ball and chain.

True forgiveness is so very liberating and is the only way to freedom. Don't allow the pain and hurt of the past to prevent you from receiving the good of your future. No person or thing should ever keep you from releasing the past and receiving the love and life waiting for you.

Forgiving yourself

Forgiving yourself is the start of understanding your complete self. Loving yourself is understanding and accepting the complete you, all the good and the not so good. Everyone has a side to them that they are not totally proud of or try to hide. But this side is also important. Learning to forgive and accept all of ourselves, even the parts that we think are bad, will open us up to seeing every part of ourselves as a gift. Even the not so good side of us can be a gift.

As a young girl I was a very independent thinker. I also would let someone know if I felt he or she was wrong. I remember when I was in third grade, the teacher handed my math test back to me. I saw that she had marked one answer I felt was correct, wrong. So I turned to my friend and told her that I thought I was right. The teacher heard me and said that if I felt I was right, I should come up to her and explain why I thought it was correct. I walked up to her desk and politely told her that I thought my answer was correct and explained why. She then told me why it was wrong and then said because I was insolent I would have to stay in for recess. I did not understand what "insolent" was and I did not understand why I was being punished. I did think that I was being punished for sticking up for myself with an adult. I was bad.

I also was almost always the leader of my group of friends. I would organize our team and delegate different jobs to different kids. One time I heard one mother talking to another. They were saying I was bossy and this was not a good quality to have. Again, I was bad.

Throughout my childhood and teen years I gathered all these so-called bad qualities. Because I wanted to be liked and do well,

I hid these qualities. If they did slip out, I would be angry with myself.

It wasn't until my 30s, when I found myself almost broke and needing a place to live, that my independent thinker quality came up with an independent idea to find a nice place to live. I told my soon-to-be landlord I would fix up the apartment if I could have two months free of rent. He said that would work. I now had a nice place to live. The so-called bad quality of being bossy has been an asset when working with anywhere from twenty-five to one hundred fifty singers as a choir director, gathering their voices into one unified sound. And the quality of sticking up for myself or asking questions if I feel something isn't right is not insolent, but rather a quality that has kept me out of trouble. All my so-called bad qualities were really good qualities that have helped me through my life. But it wasn't until I learned to accept all of me that I was able to see these undesirable qualities as assets. After I forgave and accepted all of myself, I didn't have to hide these so-called bad qualities. Now they are my gifts.

During my marriage I had to become very strong so that my family could function well during some stressful times. However, this was a quality that did not go over so well with my husband. He did not want a strong, free-thinking woman. Needless to say, it caused friction in the marriage. I would beat myself up verbally every time that side would show itself. However, I liked my free-thinking side and found it hard to hide it. When I look back objectively to the last few years of my marriage, at first I was angry that I hadn't hidden that part of me. It had just made things worse. However, it was that part of me that searched for solutions and options for my situation. It was the part of me that led me to learn more about myself, and what I needed to do to save myself. I forgave myself, but even more important I accepted myself; even my free-thinking self.

Accepting and loving all sides of yourself helps you to see your situation for what it is, learn from it, forgive, and let it go! You will be free from it. If you are too busy beating yourself up for mistakes you think you may have made or the bad qualities you showed, you will not see your situation for what it is.

If I closed my eyes to the fact that it was my strength that held our family together when times in our family were difficult, and if I only saw how later it caused friction in my marriage, I would not be seeing my situation correctly. I would be blaming myself instead of learning what really had gone wrong. And if I was so busy blaming myself, I certainly would not be able to learn from the situation or let it go.

It is time to accept yourself—your complete self—and forgive.

"Without forgiveness, there's no future."
—DESMOND TUTU

How to begin to Forgive

An ideal time to work on forgiving is during your meditations or quiet times. When you are relaxed, listening, and centered, you are able to see the whole picture more clearly and without drama. You are able to see the lessons from the situation and learn from them.

Begin as you do with your normal meditation. When you are centered and ready, look back upon your situation, back to the events that led to your prison, maybe the betrayal, hurt or some other major turning point. Then go back further, to what led to these problems. What led to the turning point for you? Be honest, open, and gentle with yourself. See the events for what they are. Do not let yourself get dragged into all the guilt or anger and confusion. It is in the past and cannot change. Accept and find the lesson from them.

Once it is crystal clear in your mind, take a deep breath and forgive yourself. Forgive yourself for whatever part you played in the story of your marriage. Forgive, learn from it, and let it go! You cannot change it. Keep the lesson you have learned and forgive yourself! Say so you can hear it: "God/Source loves me!" Let the light of forgiveness flow through every muscle. Allow the light of forgiveness push every bit of guilt and anger out of your body and mind. Fill yourself with forgiveness and love.

In a separate meditation, again think back to your situation and its end, but this time you go back to what caused your situation. What led you to not be happy? If you are having difficulty with a person, what has led to this difficulty? Instead of an accusing look, take an objective look at how the two of you hurt each other. Now take a look at the person or the situation apart from the hurtful events—the things you loved and the things you did not, all the details that make up the situation or the person. Try to look at why things happened the way they did. Why that person acted the way they did. When you are ready, "God loves ____. God loves me" and forgive them. Forgive and let them go! They are not there to hurt you anymore. Again, let the light of forgiveness flow through you and push out the hurt and anger and revenge. Out of your body it goes. Now fill yourself with the light of forgiveness and freedom.

During my divorce, I felt the need to forgive. Was this difficult? Yes, especially since our divorce was not finished and continued hurt was being thrown around. However, forgiveness was needed so I could see my situation without the mess and negative energy. Forgiving allowed me to open my heart to the possibility of us coming to an agreement and finalizing our divorce. As my heart opened to this feeling, every time I spoke to my soon-to-be-ex I did not harbor anger or resentment. Without these negative feelings, I became open to helping our kids get along with their dad, and I tried to resolve our differences instead of arguing. I also learned how to get over anger very quickly. Three-fourths of our divorce resolved through mediation and talking. This would have never happened if I was angry or trying to make him pay. Forgiveness and understanding that God/Infinite Source loved him as much as he/she loved me helped me to keep things in perspective. We really were equal in the eyes of God. I could see above the trees of the forest instead of wandering around lost in the forest.

Forgiveness for myself took a little more time. I had to look deeper and understand my own reasons for the way I contributed to the problem. Totally releasing and forgiving yourself and your situation may take more than one meditation, but it is extremely important because it is for you. You see, it is about you! You first feel how great it feels to release and forgive yourself. How the muscles relax and it is so easy to smile. Well, imagine what you will feel when you release and forgive the event, situation, or person. Imagine how it will feel not to have the tightness in your stomach, shoulders, or wherever you feel stress.

You might feel that no one deserves your forgiveness—but again, it is not about him or her. It is for and about you. You deserve to forgive and release all that anger, hurt, and guilt—none of which helps you with yourself, your family, or your future. Let it go!

So many times I hear people tell me how awful their situation was. How angry they were or are and how they fought back in mean and hurtful ways. I hear, "I will show them." Show them what, and why try to show them anything? Again, these are people who have supposedly moved on anywhere from three to twenty-five years ago. Really? Twenty-five years and they still feel the anger, the vengeance, and even worse, the need to prove something to someone who doesn't care or even to themselves for mistakes they have made. Why hold onto all this? Who is this hurting? Not the person or event they left—it is hurting them. They are not going forth into their lives and their future.

I have been divorced for two years. I do not feel any animosity towards my ex-spouse or his family. I do not care to prove anything to him. I forgive him and myself for what caused our divorce and what took place during the divorce. It is what it is and it is in the past. I took what I needed to learn from it and let go of the rest. Even if it did take several forgiveness meditations to really forgive and release. Yes, sometimes once is not enough, but it's worth it. I cannot tell you how wonderful I feel. My stomach and shoulders are relaxed and I never feel that hateful need for revenge.

I forgive both of us. The great thing is, it doesn't matter if he forgives me. It is not about him. It is, however, everything for me.

Forgiveness gives you the freedom to move forward into your wonderful life and light without the baggage to drag you down.

If I could give you a gift, the ability to allow forgiveness would be it.

If we could read the secret history of our enemies, we would find in each person's life sorrow and suffering enough to disarm all hostility.
—HENRY WADSWORTH LONGFELLOW

Forgiveness is a very big and important step. Please take your time with it and move on to the next chapter when you are ready.

Take Time to Focus:

1. If you are having trouble focusing on the events or person who wronged you, try to write it out. Write about the events, what led to them, and why. Write your part in the events; if there is another person, write about their part in the events or the hurt. Write about what was good about your situation or the person. Study what you have written. Meditate on it and forgive when ready.

2. Write down what you find are your good qualities. Now write down the qualities you want to hide. Meditate on the qualities you want to hide. When did they help you? How can you use them to be a better person? Or can you accept them for what they are?

3. If you find it hard to forgive another person try first to send loving light to them. Remember we are all equally loved in the eyes of Infinite Source/God. You may say. "God loves so and so and God loves me." It may take time and that is fine. Forgiveness is a process–allow it to flow at it's own pace.

AFFIRMATION: I, *(insert name)*, will work to forgive myself and others for and mistakes, or hurtful events. If I cannot forgive at this moment, I will keep in my mind the act of forgiveness and work towards it. I understand that only with forgiveness can I truly be free and can move on with my life in a positive way. Forgiveness is the key. Date:_____

CHAPTER 11

Every Little Thing You Do:

The Ripple Effect

Instead of worrying about the things I cannot change,
I can better spend my energy changing
and improving what I can and I watch
as it ripples and grows.

A very good friend told me I needed to take care of what was happening in my own circle, not everyone else's circle. What was she talking about? Was she implying that I was overstepping my bounds or being nosy? It took me a day to really understand what she was saying. When I finally got the "Ah-ha" moment, I realized how smart she is!

It was at the very beginning of my divorce and I was angry. I hadn't started to forgive yet. The way I vented my anger was to complain about what my soon-to-be-ex was doing to me and to our children. Complaining seemed to be the only way I could cope with the hurt I was feeling.

When my friend said I should only take care of my own circle, I thought, "My circle is great. What is she talking about?"

During or after a divorce, especially when children are involved, it becomes easy to always worry and complain about what your ex or soon-to-be-ex is doing differently than you. Or more to the point, what he or she is doing wrong. It is so easy to blame others and pick on others.

What my friend was saying is to let go of things I could not control. I will repeat this important concept again because I really want you to get it. You need to let go of things you cannot control. You may be saying, "What?" or "Not me," but take a few minutes and think about this concept. **Let go of what you cannot control.**

Could I control what my soon-to-be-ex was saying or doing at his home? Could I control the fact that I felt I always had to be the bad guy? You know, the parent who made sure homework and chores were done, while it seemed like all he did was play? Could I control this? Well, yes and no.

No, I could not control what my soon-to-be-ex was doing, but yes, I could control what I was doing and how I was feeling. Of course it is easier to blame my soon-to-be-ex and definitely doesn't take much effort. However, it isn't the truth.

I am not a victim! You are not a victim! But with this statement comes responsibility. Responsibility for where your focus lies. Responsibility for what you say and do in any situation. Responsibility for seeing where you can make a difference, making the absolute best of those circumstances. For me it was responsibility for helping my children and myself through the divorce, so everyone feels secure. When we take this responsibility we are claiming our authoritative control. That is where the ripple effect begins.

By taking the focus off what my soon-to-be-ex was doing and instead focusing on helping myself and the children handle their world turning upside down, I became proactive and responsible. I stopped living in a world of complaining and denial.

Once I began to focus on my own circle, I saw that my oldest child not only had a home life disrupted, but was also facing a hard school year with a class full of new people and one teacher with whom he particularly struggled. I saw our middle child, who at first glance seemed fine, hiding finished homework in the recycle bin, trash, or in the back of his desk instead of handing it in. Why? If I decided to simply blame my soon-to-be-ex for all this or better yet, ignore it, how would I be helping our children? How would I help them to feel that I would always be there for them? I could not!

Instead of worrying about the things I cannot change, I can better spend my energy changing and improving what I can. So I spoke with the teachers about what I had observed. I talked with each child separately and all together, always saying and showing: I am here for you, I will always support you, and we as a family will be fine. I emphasized that we as a family must pull together and support one another.

To make sure I would never forget this focus point, I wrote down what I want our children to feel about our family when they are grown and have their own families. What I want family to mean to them. Every time I have a situation I can deal with in a better way, I look at that paper beside my bed and I ask, "Am I on target?" It puts my focus back into perspective.

Taking Responsibility for Others Success

Often, people are asked to take responsibility for other people, either extended family or people on the job. Am I responsible for every person that comes into my life? Yes and no. It is my responsibility to be tolerant, open and have compassion with people and their problems. I can even present a solution or perspective on a problem they may be dealing with. However, it is not up to me to save them. That is not even possible. They must save themselves. We can offer a different perspective or plant a seed for a new way of thinking, but we cannot make that person change. They have their own lesson to learn and their own journey to travel. We can help but we cannot stop them in their own discovery. This is outside our circle.

Don't get me wrong; when friends want help or people come to me wanting to change their lives, I am there for them. I will provide them with the support, friendship, and new thoughts, concepts, and possible solutions, but I cannot make them accept these ideas or concepts. That is up to them — it is their journey. If I became totally responsible for them, I would be taking away the opportunity for them to learn their lesson and become responsible for themselves and their lives. I would be making them a victim.

A very wise person once told me that he never makes a decision for his children. He will present the "what if's" of each choice, but it is up to the child to make the choice and live with the result. Each of his children has become very successful. Why? Because they are able to make decisions with clear vision of the possibilities before them. Does this wise father take the credit for the success of his children? No, as he says, "They are responsible for their success. I simply believe in them."

The Ultimate Relief of Accepting Responsibility

This is what my friend meant by saying you can only control things in your own circle. It requires focus, claiming authoritative control for what I can control in my life, and pulling my family together with support, love, lots of listening, and always, always being totally there for them. Can I prevent every mistake they make? No, but I can be there to listen, support, and offer possible solutions. And if I see that they are traveling down a road that will create more problems, I will allow myself to intervene and present to them better options or easier and more successful routes to the same goal. Most of all, I respect them and their ability to think and decide.

Caring for your own circle takes looking with clear vision at your situation. You cannot see with clear vision if you are blaming someone or something else or even yourself for everything. Blaming takes too much focus and energy. Instead, you can look at your situation, accept and take responsibility for what you can do. I was the parent who saw what was happening to our children. They were all showing stress from our situation. If I had closed my eyes and ignored it or blamed my soon-to-be-ex, I would have missed an opportunity to address important problems. My children would not have had my support. They would still be dealing with the separation of their family on their own if I had not decided to be responsible for my own circle, offer help and control the things I could control. It is amazing how much effect we have on so many people by how we respond or decide how to treat a situation.

Taking the first step to better yourself and your situation is taking the steps towards your authoritative control. It is positive and empowering. And you will be surprised how many people will notice and be affected by your decision. Taking responsibility for how you see yourself and your relationships with other people can change your world. You can control how you respond to a person who unnerves you or tries to rattle you. Start now to think about the best way to respond when this person baits you. Now you are being proactive, responsible, and ready.

For example: A particular person always tries to bait you into an argument. Every time you try to talk to him, you end up fighting. Obviously, we cannot control his behavior or wave a magic wand and make him suddenly be nice. What we control is how we handle his behavior or anger and yelling. We can be prepared for how he will act and respond instead of reacting. We can decide how we want to handle the situation and not allow someone else to berate us. It is very hard to argue with someone who doesn't argue back.

Try this exercise with a friend: Tell the person that you are going to push against his or her hands and the person is to push back, but then let go on the count of three. But until the person lets go, you both need to push against each other as hard as you can. One, two, three, let go! What happened? Who has the control? Hopefully you see the person who let go was the one left with the control. And hopefully, no one fell.

It is the same for a verbal argument. The person who lets go, who says, "No, we can't get anything accomplished if we are yelling. Let's talk about this when we are calmer and can control ourselves," and walks away, has the control. You responded and did not react. See how it works.

This method works in our work life also. If you are having a problem with a co-worker, try to talk calmly about the situation. If the other person turns critical or tries to start an argument, politely but firmly leave the situation. Send the person love. You not only keep your personal power, but you also avoid adding anger to the situation.

If you not happy with your life or career, take a closer look at it. Can you make your situation better or do you need to make a change in your life? This is your decision. As you meditate, form a grateful heart, forgive, and learn to love your true self, the answer will become crystal clear. Be honest with yourself. What do you need to do to break away from your prison and find freedom and joy? Once you can answer this question, then you need to figure out the steps that will be best for you and everyone involved. This is taking responsibility for your life and your circle. How do you want to respond? What else can you do in a proactive, positive way to attain what you want?

It truly is up to you and no one else. You are more aware of yourself and what is truly going on around you, and you are sure of yourself and happy with who you are as a person. You have looked objectively at your situation. You have the answers within you. You realize you need to focus on the important issues you and your family face. The more you have forgiven and made the decision to break free in a positive way, the easier it is for you to see when a situation is not serving your purpose or actually working against what you want to achieve. Now you are able to rise above the mess of any situation and do what is needed to attain your goals in a positive way without getting dragged down.

What might amaze you is that in time, the person who was so angry and insulting towards you starts to become more civil and willing to discuss issues in a calm and productive manner. The insults and blame will start to minimize and slowly disappear. Again, you have taken control of what you can control and created a better situation. You have created a better life.

When my friend told me to take control of my own circle, it opened my eyes! To this day, I keep this in mind. I feel in control of how I want to be treated and how I want my life to be. I have some smart friends!

Take Time to Focus:

1. Read over the paragraph you wrote concerning your prison or situation. Take time to think, "Am I being responsible for me, for my circle?" Make a written list of proactive changes you can make to become more responsible and more in control. Keep this list beside your bed and read it in the morning to focus and at night to see what you accomplished.

2. When an unpleasant situation occurs allow yourself a pause. What do I mean by a pause? Stop and think how do I want to respond? What is the best result for this problem? What type of person do I want to be in this situation? Is this something I can change or is it out of my control?

3. As you practice this "pause", it will become habit. You will become calm, thoughtful and happier.

4. Take time to write down the results you see happening because you have taken responsibility for yourself, your situation, and your circle. How does it feel to be more in control?

AFFIRMATION: I, *(insert name)*, will, from this point on, take responsibility for the things I can control and for the life I want to have. I realize to blame everyone and everything will waste my time and energy. I alone have the ability to create my world and I alone will take responsibility for my world.

Date: _____

CHAPTER 12

What Really Makes You Tick?:

Self-Esteem

Take a look in the mirror.
Do you see the beautiful, talented person I see?
If not, you aren't truly seeing You!

Have you had everything ready to move on to your dream, only to stop yourself from acting on it. Or even started a diet that was guaranteed to work, only to find a donut in your hands. Why? Why do we sabotage ourselves? What is stopping us from doing the things we want to do?

Self-image affects everything we do and say and how we perceive our world. It affects how we relate to ourselves and others. It affects the choices we make and how we react or respond to all situations. It is what we truly believe about ourselves, deep down inside. It is the belief we hold in our subconscious mind. Our self-image determines how we see or create our reality.

Many people who run away and start over do so only to find they are running into the same problems, the same dead ends they had in their old life. Why? Because the change needed to come from within themselves first. Can you see yourself in the following situation?

Lyndi could never find a place she was happy living. During high school she would always say, "I am going to leave here. I know there is something better. You watch, right after high school, I am gone."

After high school Lyndi went to five different colleges. She would always send me messages saying, "I am moving on. I know there is something better." When she finally attained her degree she moved frequently, only staying in one place for less than two years. No matter where Lyndi moved or tried to settle she found that the same problems or issues would arise in her life. She felt unsettled and found it hard to make new friends. It was easier to pack her bags and start again with new hope and dreams.

Finally, when I received a note from her saying she was moving on yet again, I sent her a message saying, "Lyndi, maybe it is time to stop and find out what inside you can't find home." Two months later she responded to my message. She agreed she couldn't find "home," and that she was going to find out why.

Three years later she wrote me a letter. She told me she had been living in Oregon and loved it. She had friends, met a super guy and was finally home. I called her and asked what had changed? Why was Oregon the magic place? Lyndi laughed, "It isn't the place, even though it is beautiful here, it's me. I read the message you wrote me three years ago over and over. You were right. It wasn't all the different places, it was me. I needed to find out what I was running from."

Lyndi went on to tell me the process she went through to discover herself. She felt it had a lot to do with looking within herself and listening to what she truly was looking for. Lyndi told me it was security she was searching for. She had a childhood where she did not feel very secure. Her mom was always changing jobs and men. Lyndi never felt she had the home she wanted.

Take a moment to look into the mirror. What do you see? Do you see a beautiful person looking back at you? Do you see someone who feels blessed with all life has to offer? Do you see a person with a goal or purpose? Do you see someone who is determined? Do you see all the love and the compassion you have inside you? Can you say, "Yes, I have it all going on. I truly am a special, wonderful person!"

If you can answer yes to all these questions, that is great. You are developing or already have a positive self-image. If you do not see all the wonderful qualities you possess or find yourself criticizing parts of yourself as you look into the mirror, ask yourself why.

Let's start at the beginning and learn how our self-image is formed. When we are born we see beauty, goodness, love, joy, and faith in everything. We are trusting. I feel we are born with our own special purpose for being here and a lesson to learn. God/Source has made us in its image and its image is beautiful. In everything we do, we shine God's light. The world is our oyster!

As children from the ages of 1 to 6 years old, our minds are quick to absorb everything we see, touch, feel, hear and taste. Our minds, conscious and subconscious are totally open and absorbing. Through our parents, relatives, friends, TV, radio and other experiences, everything we are exposed to enters our mind, makes an impression and then gets placed into our subconscious mind. Everything we are exposed to gets absorbed into our subconscious mind and starts to form what we think about ourselves and our world. A child who enters first grade wanting to experience and explore, is curious and easily accepts friends is a child whose experiences thus far have been loving and have promoted creativity and curiosity. A child who enters first grade scared to ask questions and who doesn't want to participate, explore, or discover has had experiences that may not have been so positive. These children do not feel as sure of themselves or the world around them because of the experiences they have already absorbed.

Once we're in school, we have teachers, friends, newspapers, TV, music, and books all feeding into our minds. We are exposed to more experiences, good and bad, which will also help shape what we think of ourselves and our world. The subconscious mind cannot choose what it accepts.

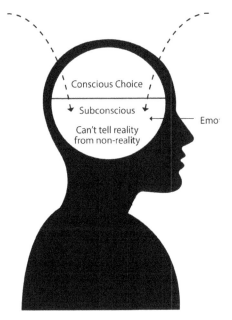

Diagram No. 1

What I find very interesting is sometimes it is a simple comment, positive or negative, from someone you trust that will stick with you the most and settle in your subconscious. There it can become the basis for the decisions you make in life.

These experiences, events and comments that make a lasting effect on us and get buried into our subconscious are called, by many, paradigms. Paradigms are beliefs hidden deep inside our subconscious. When the paradigms were formed, they were supposed to protect or help us. As we grow and events change these old beliefs or paradigms sometimes do not serve us anymore and can even keep us from living the life we want and deserve. As I have already said, some paradigms are positive and some are negative. However, both affect how we see ourselves and others and the world around us. They help to create our reality.

An example I remember as if it was yesterday involves my dad teaching me to swim. I was three years old and loving the attention and the water. I was in my glory! My dad was teaching me the sidestroke. I was all excited and said, "I can do it, Daddy!" He smiled and said, "My dear, you can do anything you truly put you mind to. There is nothing in this world you can't achieve if you really, really want it."

My subconscious grabbed hold of that comment. My dad never said it again, but he didn't need to—I had it. I truly feel that is why I always had a deep feeling of optimism and hope that has carried me through many hard times in my life.

When I was in junior high and high school, my dad started a new comment: "You are a girl and need to be taken care of and be careful." This change in his view of me caused many rifts between the two of us—and that phrase "need to be taken care of" also stayed in my subconscious and would affect my decisions in life.

I didn't say what our mind holds onto always makes sense, or that there are no contradictions within.

When I met Janet, she constantly said, "You can't trust men." It really didn't matter what we were talking about; that would always come to the surface. Finally, I had to find out why.

"Janet, surely you have a male friend or someone of the male gender that you like and trust?" I asked.

"No," she replied dryly.

"Okay, so why can't you trust them?"

"My mother always told me you can't trust them and she was right. Look at my two marriages! They both cheated," she said.

"How about your mom? Did she have a happy marriage to your dad?"

"Oh no, Mom married five times and none of them could be trusted," she answered.

So in Janet's eyes all men cheated or had affairs. Janet did not leave room for any man to be any different.

Janet knew that I had also known her soon-to-be-ex, Tom. We had all been friends for quite some time. I told her that he was very unhappy, that he was very much in love with her but he was confused. He did not know how to deal with her constant accusations that he was cheating. She had even embarrassed him at work by calling all his female colleagues and accusing them of fooling around with him. He simply could not be with someone who did not trust him. However, he adored Janet and really wanted to work everything out. I felt he was telling the truth and had not had any affairs.

Both Janet and Tom worked on themselves and with each other. Janet began to see that not being able to trust any man was a belief that was not totally accurate and was keeping her away from a good man who loved her. Slowly, they started to talk and then date. After two months and six dates, Janet came to me with tears in her eyes.

"I can't believe how I have hurt my marriage. I can't believe how I almost lost him. I knew deep down in my heart he wasn't cheating, but I couldn't stop blaming him. I was so scared of getting hurt . . . like my mom."

Janet was dealing with a negative paradigm that had settled into her subconscious when she saw her mom hurt and angry because her husband had cheated on her. Maybe her mother had simply told her no man could be trusted and that is all it took to stick with her into adulthood and alter her life.

Whatever the case, it was enough that it went into her sub-conscious and became a strong belief that would alter her perception of men and what decisions she made for her life.

Why is it so hard to change our results?

Diagram No. 2.

In diagram No. 2 you can see the top part of our mind is displayed as the conscious mind. This is the thinking, reasoning mind. It can choose what it wants to believe or not. The conscious mind then stores for a limited time the learned information. This is why you can study hard for a test in school, receive a 100% and then forget what you have learned. The lower half of the mind is shown as the subconscious mind. The subconscious mind will let everything in. It is also the area that holds

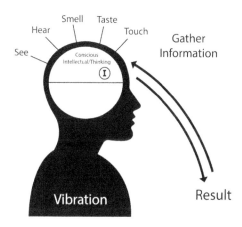

our intuition, deeper level of understanding and our paradigms — all the old beliefs that once served us but now keep us from living lives we want to live.

Many people want to change the results in their lives. For example, if I looked at the scale and saw I needed to lose 20 pounds, I would think in my conscious mind, "I will stop eating fatting, sugary foods." I may stick to my plan the first day, but the next day I find a donut or cookies in my hand. Later in the afternoon a bag of chips. Or I lose the weight only to gain it all back in six months to a year. I again look at my results and think "I have to lose this weight." But still I get the same results. This is how 97 percent of the population lives their lives. They let the results determine the action and they receive the same results.

If we want to see different results, such as finding the love of our life instead of unattainable people, then we think in our conscious mind "I want the love of my life." Because we feel this desire, it may enter into our subconscious. If it does go into the subconscious, it may quickly be taken over by a paradigm that says, "I don't deserve a happy relationship," or "I have to hide and protect my heart." So when a special person comes into our life with their heart in hand, our paradigm will not allow us to be open to this person. We end up with the same results — no love in our life. The key is to change the paradigm and replace it with the wanted desire or belief.

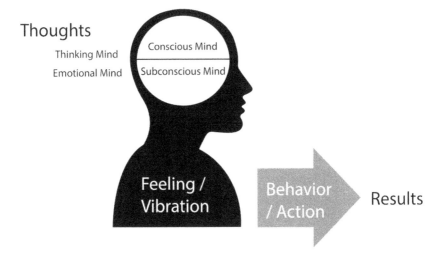

Thoughts

Thinking Mind

Emotional Mind

Conscious Mind

Subconscious Mind

Feeling / Vibration

Behavior / Action

Results

Diagram No. 3

Do you have a strong belief, a paradigm that is affecting how you see yourself and your world? Does it affect your decisions and relationships? Discovering and examining those paradigms, good or bad, is the key to opening the door to achieving your life.

Let's go back to that old paradigm of mine about needing someone to take care of me. Let's see how that can change the whole direction of my life, if I allow it.

I was so proud of myself. I had sold the house where I had lived during my marriage and had found a perfect house for our family. This new house was beautiful and my children loved it. It was the day for me to close on

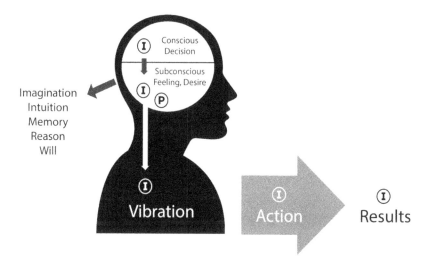

this beautiful, perfect home. I was excited because I knew this was my first step to moving on. I was rocking to the radio and had just turned onto the street where the closing was going to take place when it hit me. I heard it loud and clear. "You can't do this. You need someone to take care of you. You need someone to do this for you." I felt the fear and the doubt. I actually put the brakes of the car on and froze for a second. This old belief hadn't shown its face for so long, I thought it was gone! So there I sat, faced with a choice. Would I allow this old paradigm to scare me from moving on? Would I allow it to keep me from doing something to better my family and give me more strength and confidence? Or would I say no to this old belief and move forward?

I sat in my car and had what I call the talk. "Really? After all this time, are you really going to stop dead and not move forward? Why can't I do it? Why can't I do anything I truly want to do? Of course I can do it! I am smart, strong, and I have made up my mind. God is with me. And the

Universe will help me if needed. I do not need anyone to take care of me. I am prepared and ready! Now go inside and knock this old nasty paradigm out of the water!"

I then proceeded to the building, went in and closed on a home that has brought my family much comfort, safety, togetherness and fun. As for me, I feel stronger and yes, independent. If I truly want to do anything, I can achieve it. Watch out, negative paradigms, because here I come.

How do we uncover these negative beliefs? First, let's say to ourselves that we can achieve anything we truly put our heart and soul into achieving. There is nothing we can't do! Write this on a card and say it over and over throughout the day. At the end of the day, how does it feel? Does your heart jump up and down ready to start? Are you saying, "Well, of course I can achieve anything I truly desire." Or do you simply not believe it? Then this is the time to sit down and start writing. Write down some of the desires you have for your life and what keeps you from attaining them. Why you are not able to be who you want to be. Why relationships are not turning out the way you want them to. Write down every obstacle that comes to your mind. Try to dig a little deeper, such as: All the men/women you date are unattainable and that is why your relationships always end. Well, then, why do you choose unattainable relationships? Do you really desire to stay alone for a while? Are you scared to get too close to someone at this time? Really question yourself, and behold, a negative paradigm will show its face.

Maybe you don't want to get too close because you don't want to be hurt. Why do you feel you will be hurt? Maybe because it has happened before and you don't ever want to feel hurt again. Voila, there is the paradigm. One method to break a paradigm is to replace it with the new belief or desire by repetition. The use of affirmations is great if done a few times every day, in a mirror looking in one eye and then the other eye. The trick is to really feel or internalize a strong, positive feeling when saying the affirmation. Emotion helps your desire to grow and replaces the paradigm that believes differently.

Another way paradigms are changed is by a surprising or memorable event.

Still a third way is knowing it is a paradigm and talking it down proving it wrong by definite, immediate action. This is what I did as I sat in my car talking myself into going to the closing on my house.

Affirmations like the ones I have at the end of each chapter are also very effective in changing paradigms. The key is to totally internalize the affirmation and the meaning behind it. If the affirmation causes butterflies in your stomach, then it is the one you need to repeat.   Affirmations are best said while looking into a mirror first with one eye covered and then again with the other eye covered. Feel the outcome of believing the phrase – like it is already your belief. Say your affirmation in this way until you have changed your belief/paradigm.

Another way is more spiritual. In meditation or subconscious/spirit writing you ask these beliefs to come forward. Your mind brings forth either in picture form or written form various paradigms you may hold deep inside. With each paradigm you discover its story — your story. How did it become a paradigm? Then by understanding and reasoning you replace or modify this old belief.

I actually used this more spiritual method with a paradigm of being worthy to attain in my life. This was an old belief that life was hard and few could really make it. This came from hearing my mother speak with relatives and friends. You had to be special to make it in this world. As I went back to those conversations in meditation, I was patient with this paradigm. I gave reasons why this old belief should be changed. Slowly but surely, my belief changed to: I am the special one who can not only have what I truly desire, but I also deserve to attain my dreams. It helped to remember my dad reinforcing this when I was three years old. Now I am free of that limiting belief. I have replaced it.

The more you beat a paradigm and grow your desire through any of these methods, the smaller it becomes. Soon it disappears as the new belief takes over. How you choose to change your belief system is your choice.

Once you recognize it, you can stop it in its tracks or at least know you have a choice to break the paradigm or stay with it.

It is your choice.

It is important to realize that all of the above methods of changing paradigms involve deep feeling, reinforcing your desire and allowing it to grow. If you do not feel strongly about your dream, then chances are you won't be able to remove the paradigm for good.

You were put on this earth to achieve something wonderful. You truly are a special person with your own unique and important gifts. God, the Universe or the Ultimate Infinite Source has put you here to shine! You were put here to have a beautiful chance to be whatever is waiting inside you to emerge. Whatever your gift or whatever your true desire is, now is the time to be and live it. No one else on this beautiful earth of ours knows who you truly are and what you truly have in your heart. Only you! Why else would you be here? Do you want to live your life without achieving the life you know you want or be the person you know you are inside and want to be on the outside? Does it truly make sense that we were put on this earth to achieve nothing? To waste our time and die with regret? To me this makes absolutely no sense. Why not just stay in heaven? Life is a gift from above. A gift is not supposed to be wasted. So what is holding you back? Your life is a gift. You are a gift. Be thankful for the awesome chance to make the very most out of your life, your gift. I truly believe in my heart and soul that each one of you is a very special person. Yes, you have your own special light to shine. I know that you have a special purpose that will help the world and make it a better place.

Now is the time for you to totally open up to your true self and your desires for your life. It is time to rid yourself of all the blocks of ideas, concepts or paradigms that keep you away from creating your love of life. Start by make a plan for how to get started on achieving these desires and begin to move towards your life. The time is now!

The plan need not be complex. In fact, the simpler it is, the easier you can act on making your desire a reality. Once I decided to change my "not worthy to attain" paradigm, I made the plan to write out every time in the history of my life I attained my goal. I found I had quite a few achievements I never gave myself credit for achieving. It was a simple plan, but very effective in forming a new belief that I am more than worthy and capable of attaining my dreams.

As you move toward your desires there will be moments like when I was buying my new home—times where self-doubt, fear and those awful, negative paradigms appear to try and stop your progress. They can be very convincing. They have stopped you before and if you let them, they will stop you again. The key is to recognize them and stop them. You must believe in your desires of what you want your life to be, who you want to be as a person and how you want your relationships with others to be from now on. Once you realize that the fear, doubt, and negative paradigms happen anytime you are making a change in your life, you can deal with them. This is what I did as I sat in the car telling myself I can do it! I can achieve what I truly desire. I can be the strong, self-reliant, and confident woman I desire to be, and no negative paradigm is going to stop me.

The funny part is that now that I have recognized and dealt with this negative paradigm it becomes easier and easier to dismiss it. Every day I become more of the person I know I am. My life is becoming more the life I want to live and the purpose for my life is happening. The very first step was writing this book: to help others realize and step away from their prisons with confidence, purpose and to move on with the life that awaits them. To give people their voices back and help them to sing. I am creating my own reality. My world and I am fulfilling my purpose!

Your life is waiting for you. What you want is glorious. So, what are you waiting for?

Take Time to Focus:

1. As I suggested in this chapter, look into a mirror at yourself. Try to tell yourself you are beautiful or handsome. Can you congratulate yourself for who you are? Can you see yourself for all the goodness you have inside you? Can you see your own bright light? If you cannot see how truly wonderful you are as a person, then write down how you see yourself now in one column. Across from this column write down how you want to see yourself. Write something positive to offset every negative feeling you have stated in the previous column. The third step is to write in short sentences below how you are going to change the negative into the positive. What actions can you take to change your negative beliefs to positive?

2. After a week of focusing on number one of "Take Time to Focus," move on to number two. Find a quiet moment and relax. When you are ready begin to think back to moments you did not know why you did what you did. Why did you sabotage your diet, your career, or a success in your life? What belief or paradigm is keeping you in your prison? Why do you believe this? Is it time to change it? If so, read through "Invictus" listed in chapter two on responsibility. Ask yourself why any old paradigm is going to keep you from your goal, your purpose.

3. Copy the affirmation below and keep it in your pocket. Make sure you say it a few times a day. Say it with belief.

AFFIRMATION: I, *(insert name)*, believe in me. I can attain anything I truly desire and I alone can choose what I want to believe. I am the master of my life and I will fulfill my purpose. Look out, paradigms that do not serve me well. Here I come!

Date:_____

CHAPTER 13

Loving You

In All Your Glory:

Self-Love
Loving yourself is not an ego trip.
As a matter of fact, ego has absolutely
nothing to do with
loving yourself

Forgiveness and letting the past be what it is will give a wonderful sense of freedom. Freedom to accept yourself for who you truly are. Freedom to be who you want to be. Freedom in your feelings, emotions, thoughts, and actions. Most of all, freedom to love yourself.

Maya Angelou said it best when she told an old African saying: "Be careful when a naked person offers you a shirt." Loving and having compassion for yourself allows you to have greater capacity to love and give compassion to all life. You have the shirt, so share it.

Loving yourself is not an ego trip. As a matter of fact, ego has absolutely nothing to do with loving yourself. Ego is shallow and insecure. An ego constantly needs to be reassured. It is fragile, not grounded on anything but flattery. Ego always needs to feel better than or different from. It isolates us and often feels threatened.

Loving yourself is a much deeper understanding of our connection to the whole. It is being open to everything around you and accepting the others' differences. Feeling connected to everyone and everything gives us a new respect for others and ourselves. You at the very least realize everyone and everything is equivalent, although not identical. The knowledge that God or the Universe made us in his/her/its own image, gave us the Divine Energy/Soul that connects us to each other and the Universe seeing that we are all extraordinary and unique, but are living together in this wonderful world.

I have a wonderful story of connection to share with you. I was visiting the mountains in California and decided to rise early in the morning and take a hike. It was a sunny but crisp morning and I could see my breath. As I walked the path up the mountain, I often stopped to stand astonished at the beauty. Almost to the top of the mountain I came upon a grouping of Sequoia Trees. I was in awe of their stature and strength. Immediately I nestled in with these amazing trees, closed my eyes and felt the energy. The feeling of connection was immediate and strong. I felt peace and beauty. All around me I heard birds, and animals moving in the brush. The feeling of connection was profound. When I was ready to go I made sure to send loving light around all life on the mountain. I opened my eyes to see two small sparrows on the ground in front of me. I began to walk down the mountain and these two little birds hopped right in front of me chirping away. I even found myself chatting back at them. Half way down the mountain there was a huge flat rock. It looked so inviting with the morning sun shining on it, I had to lay myself right on top and warm my body. I must have dozed off. When I awoke I found little animals all around. There were more birds, a fox, squirrels and chipmunks. It was as if the mountain life was happy to have me. The feeling of connection was immense. To this day I treasure the magical moment I had on that mountain and the gifts all life gave to me.

At home I have my favorite meditation to remind me how connected we all are. I like to call it my Meditation of Oneness; while I am totally relaxed, I allow myself to open up to spirit or infinite source and feel one with every living thing. It is incredible. There is a total feeling of peace, being centered and connected. It has made me realize I am so much bigger; we are all so much bigger than the problems we may be having. Every time I do this meditation I am filled with love. It is a peaceful, calm, and accepting love. I am part of the bigger picture. I am connected.

This meditation puts everything in perspective. It allows me to see the whole picture, what truly is important, and what life is really about. This meditation is a gift.

Because I have experienced this feeling of love for everyone and everything, it stands to reason I should love myself. I am part of everyone and everything. We are all segments of the same. I tend to simplify the way I consider oneness. We all come from one Infinite Source of energy. The energy splits to every living thing. Because it is from one source, each strand contains all the qualities of one universe. Each strand carries through our DNA all evolution of life from Infinite Source/God. Even more amazing is that each of our minds has the capability of realizing any thought or idea in the past, present, or future.

This is huge. You are capable of infinite possibilities, especially if you come from an intention of love and the betterment of all. You contain all that each and every living thing contains. You have the Universe running through you. No one is better or less than anyone else. We all have definite traits we choose to emphasize; however, we all have the same traits within us. By choosing certain traits, we are allowing our own light to shine. It makes us who we are. Because you select the traits you want to accentuate, you can be whoever you want to be.

Mona is a very good friend of mine. She is close to eighty years old and has led a giving and fulfilling life. Her childhood was not a fairytale. Her mother, the primary caregiver, was abusive and mentally ill. Her father spent most of his time in bars or behind bars in prison. Mona was forced to learn how to survive while still very young, and by the time she was in high school, she was dealing drugs and living on her own.

At age 23, Mona became pregnant. This was Mona's "enough is enough" point. She did not want her child to have the same type of childhood that she had endured. She wanted to give her child more. This was the point where Mona turned her life around. She enrolled in business courses at a local vocational school and approached local businesses to see if she could be an apprentice. One business took her up on her offer and Mona started to learn a trade. By age 25 she was running the business, and by age 32 she had opened her own store.

I met Mona later in her life. Most people would say she has always had it good. If you ask her, she would say she is the most blessed person in the world. She has three successful children and a husband who loves her very much. I have never heard Mona say anything negative about another person or her life. "Everything happens for a reason," she always says.

I once asked Mona what she decided at that "enough is enough" moment. She replied, "I knew that if I wanted my child to have a better life, I had to make my life better. I had to change how I thought, my situation and who I wanted to be."

Buoyed with that immense desire to give her child a better life, Mona would not take no for an answer. After developing a plan, she acted to change her attitude and life immediately. There was no turning back. She looked to the Universe and chose what she wanted. Why not? The choice is ours alone.

Realize that the Universe or God is full of love, joy, goodness, beauty, and truth all for us, and we are all one coming from that Ultimate Source. We are meant to grow and create a world out of this extension of the source. We are meant to be everything we can be, to be truly happy and full of love for ourselves and our world.

It is usually the ego that separates us. The ego that says we are different from another group or class of people. Ego tries to elevate oneself above another. Ego and learned judgment promote prejudice and separatism. In order to raise itself higher or be more important, ego must make something or someone else inferior. I am not superior because I am white and you are African American or Indian or Chinese; or I wear glasses and you do not. I love Italian food and you might like Indian food. I might be liberal and you might be conservative. In truth, we are all one because we are from one source. We are equal. Because of this we can not only love ourselves; we can love and accept everyone.

It is hard to describe the incredible feeling of being one with all and loving yourself. A certain trust comes with the feeling. It is a strong sense of knowing that through this love, you will be guided to experiences that will benefit you. There is no room for fear or doubt. Anything is possible. It was through the Meditation of Oneness that I learned my true purpose to help others achieve happiness and purpose in their lives. It allowed me to see how small the problems we choose to create really are and how very silly it is to argue. Knowing we are all connected opens us to deep compassion, respect and love for all life around us. We understand how our actions affect everything around us. We feel the support and love of the whole universe surround us. Why would we not love ourselves when we are part of the whole wonder of Infinite Source?

When we understand this amazing truth, it becomes easy to let go of the ego. We begin to see ego for what it is; fragile and not real.

I have known Doug for over fourteen years. He is handsome, extremely talented in his profession but filled with ego. The first time I met Doug, I walked away. He was in the process of telling everyone how he was the only one who could make his boss happy. He had more sales than anyone he had ever met. Later that evening, we bumped into each other at the buffet.

"You're Alena, aren't you? Didn't you help my friend John change his life around?" he asked.

"I do know John. He is a very nice person." I answered. After my divorce I volunteered for an organization that helps families going through divorce. John was a student in one of my classes.

"Well, I was wondering if maybe we could talk . . . He has said some good things about you. I was thinking maybe you could help me." His voice was soft and I could tell he was at a turning point in his life. Obviously, he wasn't as sure of things as he had led everyone else to believe.

I agreed to talk with him and offer to help, if I could. Doug was unhappy. He did not like his job and did not feel as confident as he seemed. His wife and family didn't seem to understand him and he had started to drink way too much.

I asked him what he really wanted in life. What did he feel was his purpose? What would he love to get up every morning to do?

He closed his eyes, smiled, and said, "I want to own my own hardware store. You know, a place where all the guys hang out just to shoot the breeze and everyone comes to get whatever they need. Yeah, I have been thinking a lot about this . . . I'm just not sure if I can do it."

"Why? What is stopping you? It sounds like a wonderful idea."

"Well, I seem to be all looks and no brains," he said.

Doug's ego was a shield for the insecurity he felt about his intelligence. I told him the story of Henry Ford, founder of Ford Motor Company. I told him that Ford did not have a college education; in fact he left home and school at age 16 to work for Mr. Edison, the inventor of the light bulb. Mr. Ford then invented the first gas-powered horseless carriage. In 1899, he started the Henry Ford Motor Company. Later, he also founded the Ford Motor Company. Mr. Ford revolutionized mass production methods. In

1913 his large car production plants were the first to have moving assembly lines. Mr. Ford knew what could be. He knew it was possible to travel without a horse and he developed ways to make this happen. Mr. Ford did not listen to the sayings "You can't" or "it can't be done." No criticism would limit his desire and what he knew deep inside was possible. There were times when people thought him crazy or at least very driven. Mr. Ford saw what could be and he was not taking no for an answer.

During World War I he was brought to court as a "stupid pacifist." He was far from stupid because he knew how to pull together and organize knowledge. Mr. Ford had a desire and no one or anything was going to get him off track. He was focused and knew how to surround himself with the people who could help him make his dream a reality.

Doug and I talked for the next few weeks and he started to read about Ford, Andrew Carnegie, and other men who accomplished great things. He had started to meditate and visualize himself achieving his goal. He was feeling more confident in his idea, but still had a hard time thinking he was smart enough. I explained to him how we are of one energy and that the universe is filled with all the answers of the past, present, and future. The knowledge we need to make our dreams a reality is all around us. We just have to know how to listen. Together we did the oneness mediation. Even I was amazed with what he realized and how it helped him believe in himself.

"I can't believe it. I really can have my dream. I can fix my life. There is no reason why I should wait. The answers truly are there for me."

From that point on, there was no turning back because Doug saw all the possibilities. He understood that we all have the ability to achieve and live the lives we know we should be living. As Doug said, "We just have to get out of our own way and work with the Universe."

From that point on, Doug not only knew he could achieve his dream; he took responsibility to make it happen and to change his relationship with his family. He loved life and he loved who he had become.

You don't find Doug boasting anymore. You do find a very happy man with a wonderful hardware store filled with people.

You might be thinking, "Sure, Alena, sounds like a fairy tale." I can assure you it is not. Anything is possible. What Doug finally did was believe in himself and the Universe, make a decision, and act on it. It took seeing that he was connected to everything and with love, the answers were all waiting.

Yes, I do love myself. I love knowing what I am capable of bringing and doing on this earth. The possibilities are endless. I have the freedom to be whoever I want to be at any time. You have this same freedom. This knowledge alone can free you. Grant yourself the freedom to be whatever you want to be. The ideas are there for you to explore. You have freedom to be you. Love yourself because you are part of a whole wonderful source. How could we not love ourselves? How could we not believe?

Loving yourself in this way gives you a very strong sense of freedom, confidence, and strength. All of this comes from love. There really aren't any limitations. Anything is possible.

You owe it to yourself and everyone you come in contact with to love yourself in this way and to love others as you love yourself. We are one.

Take Time to Focus:

1. Take a walk in nature. Feel the calming, peaceful strength of the life around you. Allow yourself to feel the connection. Return love to all life.

2. Reinforce this feeling of connection with the Oneness Meditation: Relax and open your mind to the Ultimate Source/God. It may take a couple of tries, or you might do it the very first time. If you are having trouble, use music, bells, nature sounds or whatever helps to raise your vibration and relax you. Remember being grateful and full of praise also raises your vibration. Allow yourself to feel connected to every- thing. Start small and feel connected

to what is around you, who is around you. Feel the energy around you from every living thing. Then widen the circle to include your neighborhood, city, state, country, even the world. Send love to everything and allow yourself to go higher with love. Write down what you felt.

3. Do the same meditation. Start out the same but as you rise up, allow yourself to see the possibilities—all the possibilities you can achieve being connected to this vast, awesome Universe. Feel the strength, love, confidence, and purpose.

AFFIRMATION: I, *(insert name)*, am so happy and grateful that I am connected to all living creation by one loving source. I rejoice in being a part of a magnificent whole. And I am grateful for the boundless ideas, opportunities, and blessings brought to me every day.

Date: _____

BOOK FOUR
Purpose

You can have anything you want if you want it badly enough.
You can be anything you want to be,
do anything you set out to accomplish
if you hold that desire with singleness of purpose.
—ABRAHAM LINCOLN

CHAPTER 14

Living the Good Life:

Desire

*Anyone who accomplishes any type of greatness
begins with a deep desire.
There is no other way to go.
This desire is the only way; it is the purpose.
Nothing else will do.*

All success and achievement start with that one powerful all encompassing word – desire. Strong desire creates strong results. Weak desire results in weak or no results. It is up to us to feed the desire, build it and act on it. We are the only ones to give it strength and growth.

Anyone who accomplishes any type of greatness begins with a deep desire. There is no other way to go. This desire is the only way; it is the purpose. Nothing else will do.

What if you do not know your purpose or desire? How do you begin to find out why you came on this earth? Does everyone have a desire or purpose? What if you don't have anything you want to achieve? Relax. There is no need for feeling stressed or that you are missing out. Not everyone has a burning desire. Some people do not even remember how to daydream. They would not know what to do if you said, "Live your purpose or make your dreams come to life."

Yes, everyone is born for a reason. There is always a purpose. Often, people will ignore their purpose or desire because of parents who push them into doing what they think they should do or the desire doesn't seem practical or easy to obtain. Understanding that the whole purpose for us here on this planet is to allow ourselves to evolve naturally while involving a reason or desire. Sometimes we really do not know our desire. As we begin to listen to our inner selves and use our gifts like imagination and intuition, our desire/purpose will begin to reveal itself. If you are still not sure, there are methods of discovering what it is that makes your heart sing.

One very successful method is waking each morning with, "What do I want to do for me today?" At first it will be things you simply never allowed yourself to have time to enjoy; however, after a few mornings of these types of activities, a yearning to do something deeper starts to develop. Maybe you want to write a poem or story, or you want to volunteer in a particular organization, or maybe you begin to study something you have always been interested in. Whatever it is in time begins to grow and evolve, first into an idea and then a desire.

I never thought I would be an author, let alone a bestselling author. I had worked very hard since the age of 15 to have a career in music. But all I wanted to do after I dropped the children off at school in morning was to go to a coffee shop and write about everything I was learning and how it was working in my life. Any morning that I missed this one- to two-hour oasis, I felt out of sorts. Something was missing.

The more I wrote the more the different lessons started to form chapters. One day I was arguing with my computer when a man at the other end of the table asked me if I was an author. This was a defining moment. I had a choice. If I answered "no," that would allow me to stay in a safe little box of not doing anything more but write notes, but if I answered "yes", I was walking through an invisible door and becoming an author. I smiled at the man and answered, "Yes, I am. This is my first book." The man turned out to be a published author and my first writing mentor. It is as if the Universe was saying, "Are you ready? Because if you are ready to be an author, we will supply you with help to achieve your desire." But I had to step up to the plate. I had to make the decision.

Another way to discover your desire is to daydream or use your imagination. Find some time to sit under a tree or walk in a park. Begin to dream of a life you would love to live. If you aren't sure, try different scenarios. Have fun thinking of all the possibilities. One will strike your fancy and you will find yourself thinking about it more and more until it plants itself firmly in your mind and becomes your desire.

Once an idea becomes a desire there is no going back. It will nudge you and begin to grow bigger in your mind. More and more possibilities will present themselves the more you entertain the idea.

The more a person thinks or acts on his idea, the bigger it grows, until it becomes a part of the person. Every visionary with whom I have spoken always talks as if his dreams and visions are a reality in the present time. The inventor talks as if his concept is already invented. There is a reason for this. When we are on the journey to making our desire our reality, it becomes our reality as we grow into our desire. As we believe more in the ability to create our desire, we become the person living that desire.

When you have reached the point of "enough is enough" and desire change, you must allow this desire to enter into your very core and devise a solid plan to attain it. As it enters into your being it becomes solid – an inner faith begins to form that this desire will happen. But first you must make a decision to take on this desire, just as I had to say "yes" to step into the role of an author.

Debra works in a job she despises. Her life is ruled by this job. While the job pays well, it leads nowhere. When I met Debra, she had a desire to open a coffee shop in her town. Debra is very smart, personable, and full of ideas; however, I never got the sense that she had made definite, solid plans to get started on her desire to open the coffee shop. The coffee shop was a way to escape her job; however, it was not her true desire. Every time I mentioned getting some plans together, she would change the subject or come up with more ideas. But when she spoke about her job, she wanted out.

Six months later I ran into Debra and asked her if she ever opened her coffee shop.

"No, my job gave me a raise and it just seemed so hard to get it started. I guess I just need to stay where I am for now," she smiled weakly.

I asked her if she was happier staying in her job now that she had the raise. She was not happy at all, but she was scared to change. Would she be able to do well in business? How would she get the funding? I asked her if she would like me to help her. I could be there to offer tools and any help or accountability. She perked up and agreed to give it a try.

We started with a simple affirmation: "I deserve and can have the life of my dreams." Debra would say this affirmation every morning and night, and during the day when she felt she needed it.

During meditations, she looked inside to see what her purpose or true desire for life should be. To raise her vibration along with opening her mind, she began to practice being grateful, forgiving, and tolerant.

Because we have opened our minds and our hearts, it is much easier to meditate or visualize, using our inner guidance to show us our purpose or desires. We have learned and come to know all sides of ourselves — the good and what we once thought was not so good. We have forgiven ourselves and those who may have hurt us. All of this opens our hearts and minds to our passions and what really matters to us. Actually forgiveness is said to break all the chains that keep us in the past. Forgiveness is an important aspect of the Law of Creation.

If meditation is not giving you the clarity you need to discover your passion, try writing the question, "What is my desire/passion?" on a piece of paper. Put the paper in the middle of a table. Every time you walk by the table, write down something you love to do in your spare time. It may be writing poetry, carpentry, working with kids, photography, or whatever else puts the light in your eyes. Now for the next few days, focus your thinking on doing one of these things. Maybe on Monday you write a poem. How does that make you feel? Are you excited? After you write the poem, how do you feel? Could you stay and write more? Could you see yourself spending two hours writing every day? Try each of the items you listed on your paper and see which one comes alive for you. You can see yourself rejoicing every day to have a chance to do this one thing.

In three weeks' time, Debra was very excited. She knew in her heart what she wanted and needed to have the life of her dreams and wanted to help others find their life dreams. Her desire and purpose was to be a life coach. On her own, she began to plan every detail.

Before I knew it, she had a website and business cards. Shortly after that, she quit her job. There was no turning back. Debra was going to make the life of her dreams.

Six months later, her business had gotten so successful, she needed to hire someone to help answer emails. Now Debra always smiles and loves her life.

Although Debra wanted to leave her job very much, she did not have a deep desire to open a coffee shop or belief that she could have the life of her dreams. She first had to believe she could have that life and then open up to find her true purpose, her desire. Only by looking inside herself did she find what her true purpose or desire was. She wanted to help people find their purpose in life.

The combination of desire, faith that it will happen and a definite plan can make the difference between success and false start. This is key. It is the burning desire, faith in yourself and your desire, knowing it will happen and a definite plan to begin the process. These three components move you from a life of unhappiness to happiness, purpose and infinite possibility. It is often within the first couple of steps that we stop. However, if you have these three components powerfully entrenched within you, you will not fail.

Dr. Martin Luther King Jr. had a burning desire to see equal rights and social justice for all people. His desire was so strong it led him from a relatively comfortable role as a church pastor to nonviolent protests, marches, and speeches that helped to turn the tide for civil rights in America. The well-known "I Have a Dream" speech expressed his desire to "Let freedom ring" and for everyone, whether black, white, Protestant, Catholic, or Jewish to come together and be brothers.

Dr. King could have thought, "This race thing is just too big. I could never make a big enough effect. How do I even get started? How will I get the people behind me?" However, he knew things had to change. He knew that somehow, someway he was going to make a difference.

Because of Dr. King's desire for equality among all people, the opportunities to make a change came to him. This is important. The desire becomes a part of you. It has to, because you see it as happening; you start to live it. The Universe will answer and present the opportunities for you to create what you desire.

My friend Becky would always say she knew her perfect match was just around the corner. I would laugh and ask her what he looked like; his likes and dislikes; what type of food did he like, etc. I asked her all sorts of questions, and she would consistently have answers.

About one month later I was sitting in a restaurant when I saw Becky with a gentleman friend. She introduced him as her perfect match. Although he did not look exactly like she had described, he did have many similarities in his character and personality. He had the "special spark in his eyes" that Becky knew he would have. "It is as if we always have known we were meant for each other," she told me. She had the man of her dreams. They are now married with two children and very happy.

Both women allowed the desire to grow. Debra had a desire to work as a life coach. It was not just a simple want or need; it was a pulsating, living desire. She had completely internalized this desire and now was becoming the life coach she dreamed of being. It was in her conscious and subconscious. Becky had total faith that the perfect soul mate was coming to her. Everything about Becky was already with her perfect match; her thoughts and actions were as though she already had her perfect match. So her perfect match had to appear. It is her world, her creation. It is making the decision, having firm faith that it will happen and the persistence to walk towards your desire that wakes the Universe and allows it to bring you the possibilities and opportunities to make it all a reality. This is the Law of Attraction.

By having the faith and walking toward our desire we are on the vibration of making our dreams our reality. Law of Attraction states that like draws like. If we think and believe that we are something and we walk as if we are something then we are something and the Universe brings everything we need to us to make it happen.

Once I made the decision to be an author, I began to imagine my life as a writer. What would my days be like? What type of things would I really like to write about? How would I feel staying home and writing? How would I feel when someone read my writing? The more I imagined, the more real it became. Soon I was home enjoying my writing time. Now people are reading my writing. I have created my world. My imagination helped me to internalize my desire. Once my whole self is believing the desire, then it will happen. There is no other way it can go.

The problem is that many people will stop the desire before it can develop or they can start living it. It starts with doubt or fear. "What makes me think I could write a book?" Or, "What will people think if I am staying home writing? They will say it's not a real job." Now the desire is simply not a good idea and I let it slip away. Think of all the possibilities out in the Universe waiting for us to take them and create our lives. Nothing is impossible if you have the courage and faith to believe.

Look at the world around us. We talk into a little box called a cell phone. This cell phone connects to everywhere in the world. Someone thought of this idea. Someone had this idea become their desire. They allowed this desire to grow and soon they knew it could be done. They just had to figure out how.

We always feel that people who achieve these magnificent dreams are different or magical. We even put them on pedestals as if they are above us because they were brave enough to go after their ideal desire. Why? We can do the exact same thing. We can be just as successful, have the love of our life, live with joy every day, or create something that betters humanity or our world. Imagine if planes were nonexistent just because the Wright brothers decided their dream was silly. What if Thomas Edison gave up after the fiftieth experiment out of hundreds of experiments? To this day we would not have electricity.

Our dreams are given to us. It is as if the Universe is saying, "This is your way of making something magnificent in life." Yet, so many of us let these gems slip through our fingers because it isn't logical, won't be accepted, or we don't feel smart enough, strong enough or don't know where to begin. Take the first step. That is all you need to do. First one step then a second step and before you know it, you are walking your dream.

I tend to be an idea machine. Ideas come to me all day long. You may say, "Wow, she is so lucky." With all the ideas flying in my head, it can be hard to grab hold of one. If one idea grabs my attention, then I have to visualize myself creating, becoming, or achieving this idea. Even then I may not decide it's my path. The decision of my journaling turning into a book was an idea that started with enjoying the idea of having my morning tea, sitting among other people, listening to the music and writing was perfect for me. I could not wait to get to the coffee shop. It did not matter if my writing became a book for others to read or memories for me to keep sacred. It was my time to do what I enjoyed. However, when opportunities came for me to step into the author role, I took them. It seemed natural and fun.

So what gets you excited to jump out of bed and start your day? What do you find yourself doing whenever you have free time? This could be your desire or purpose.

The world is always looking for new and creative ideas. More thinking outside the box is needed in our society; dreamers are needed — especially dreamers who create their desires and make them happen.

Dreams and desires do not come when your head is crowded with negativity, doubt, fear, anger, or revenge. There isn't any room to create dreams or to foster desires when your heart is full of wrath. You can't develop your desire if you fear the criticism of others, and you can't succeed if you are in the habit of quitting when an obstacle appears. For you to be able to see your dreams and desires, you need to open your mind to all the beauty, goodness, love, faith, and joy the universe has to offer. You need to listen to the guidance of your intuition. Only then you will see the opportunities.

The most awesome journey we can have is making our dreams our reality.

All, if not most, successful people either came from difficult starts in life or came through a bad experience or crisis. That is when you open yourself up to discovering your mind. Some even call this the baptism into our "other selves." When everything seems hopeless, you feel confused and you can't take it anymore, you look for answers you never had to look for. You become open to new ways of thinking.

Changing your situation, escaping your prison and creating your future takes desire that weathers any obstacle and prohibits turning back or failure. It's a desire you can see, feel, and taste; it's a part of you. This is the desire that will take you out of your prison and lead you to your magnificent life. What are you waiting for?

Take Time to Focus:

1. What is your desire? What is it that you have to do that is part of you? Write it down on a piece of paper, linking yourself to the desire. For example: "I am so happy and grateful that I am now a _____." Or "I am so happy and grateful now that I am able to create_____."
    Carry this with you at all times. Repeat it often, especially when looking in a mirror. Believe yourself already in possession of the goal. How do you feel? Do this for a month or as long as it takes.

2. If you are not sure what your desire is, write down the things that make you happy. What makes your heart sing when you think of it? You may come up with one or more. As you meditate, practice gratefulness and forgiveness your purpose will reveal itself.

3. Having trouble finding your desire/purpose? Relax! Find time to daydream. Allow your mind to explore ideas you like and can see yourself doing. Or take a day to do only the things you want to do. What are you enjoying the most? Is it a hobby, something you haven't done in a long while? Or join some groups that help you explore your talents. If you like writing, then join a writer's discussion group. Start to explore and dream.

4. If you feel you are someone who fears, doubts, habitually quits, or is prone to laziness, write these down. Next to each one, write

how you are going to combat it. You are in control and you can conquer anything you desire to conquer.

AFFIRMATION: I, *(insert name)*, have my desire to_____

_____

_____. This desire is my creation and I will allow it to grow. I do not know exactly how it will happen, but I know it will happen. I am so happy and grateful now that I am _____

_____.

Date:_____

CHAPTER 15

So What's Stopping You?:

Fear

*Sometimes we will be all ready to move forward on our desire
when something will stop us in our tracks.
Some fear we did not even know we had will appear
causing us to run back into our comfort zone.*

Sometimes we get a desire and can really see it happening, then all of sudden we stop. Our minds fill with the "Are you crazy?" thoughts, or our friends, neighbors, or family say, "Are you crazy?" Then the doubt sets in and before you know it, your desire dies.

It is important to know this happens to many people. It is called fear or "the terror barrier". There are at least three or four basic fears that are well known. These fears can totally handicap you and your desire if you do not realize that you have the power to break through the terror barrier and conquer any fear.

Michael is a friend of mine. Every day he is thinking of what he is capable of achieving. The desires of owning a business, rising up in his company, or being an actor are all right at his fingertips. As soon as he begins to act on his dream, he comes up with reasons why he cannot let these dreams live. He lists reasons left and right why everything is impossible. These are his fears. He says it is common sense or being practical, but when do these thoughts of so-called common sense stop being common sense and instead keep you in your prison?

We often put our desires aside because we feel we are being practical or the desires are impossible. And yet, we see people achieve their dream more now than ever before because of social media. Why do these achievers not have the fears we have? Why do they not feel the limitations we feel?

The fears that stop us in our tracks are common to all. The blessings come to those who either recognize the fear and let it go or do not even allow the fears to enter their consciousness. Their desires are too strong — they have become their desire. They can't even imagine life without living their desire.

A list of the common fears that stop us in our tracks:

1. Fear of failure
2. Fear of non-acceptance
3. Fear of success
4. Other paradigms that sneak in

Fear of failing and all the negative noise that fills our heads every time we try to make a dream come to life, instead keeps us stuck. You know the thoughts; "Why do you think you can do this?", "Are you out of your mind?", "You aren't trained for this! This takes schooling." and "Why do you think you can do better than everyone else?"

Do these sound familiar? If we dig past these very common phrases to what is deeper — it is the fear of failing. Our society takes a harsh look at failure. I remember as a child when a very rich man in our town came upon hard times and lost his money. The adults were so quick to say, "You see, you can't have it good forever." "He got what he deserved. No one person should have that much money." Everyone seemed so pleased with this person's troubles. Even at a young age I thought this was strange because in the same breath they would talk about what they would do if they had that much money.

We fear what others will think, but even more we fear what we will feel about ourselves if we fail. Our whole being is defined by what we achieve. It is better to play it safe and not do anything different.

My friend Rochelle knows all about the power of fear. At one time, Rochelle just knew that if she could open an ice cream parlor in the center of their very small tourist town, it would be wildly profitable. As soon as she voiced her dream than her negative thoughts kicked in: "But it would take more money than I have to open it." "I have never owned a business. I don't know what I am doing." Rochelle was afraid of failing. Five years later there is still no successful ice cream parlor in a popular small tourist town.

But fear of failure is not the only fear to stop people from living their dreams. Another fear that is very prevalent in our society is the fear of criticism. We fear what others may think of us. "They will think I am crazy."

Actually this does have some historic value. For years, people grouped together in communities in order to survive the harsh climate. People found safety and could accomplish more when they worked together. Also, we are social animals because our energy/souls are connected. In our early communities, everyone had a particular job. There were bakers, blacksmiths, etc. These particular jobs were handed down through the family. If your father was the owner of the general store, you would also be the owner when he retired or became too old. The community depended on you doing your job, because no one else would fill the need. And because this community was all you knew, you wanted to be accepted. It is hard to not be accepted or to be pushed away.

Now in our present time, we have more opportunity and freedom to become what we want in our lives. But we still often do what we are told — be the doctor, lawyer, teacher, or fireman. We are scared of not being accepted in our community, our family. This is why there are so many people at the age of 30 to 50 that are unhappy with their profession. What if they chose a career that they were excited about? How would they feel then?

Arthur teaches high school. He loves it! Every day he comes home from work excited and full of all the things that made his day wonderful. Each child was special to him and he loved seeing them accomplish and grow.

Life was not always so happy and full of purpose. Arthur had gone to law school; he came from a long line of lawyers and was expected to follow in their footsteps. He really did try to make it work. He started to practice, switched firms two or three times but still felt something big was missing. He was not having fun. Every morning he dreaded going to the office. He knew inside himself that he belonged working with kids. He loved to see them learn and grow. One morning he simply took a big breath and said, "I am moving on."

Now, Arthur feels he is living his dream. Even though Arthur is an excellent and well-loved teacher, people of the community still gossip. "Why did he give up being a lawyer? He must not have been very good. Why be a teacher? That pays only half as much — if you're lucky."

If Arthur listens to this pointless, negative chatter, you would not know it. While all these people only do what is expected and limit themselves to what seems to be important to others, he is off living the life he wants to live. Even better, because he loves his job and the kids, the kids love him. He is a positive role model in a child's life. What could be more fulfilling?

It is no surprise that we are happiest doing what we know deep inside is our purpose. This knowing is our spirit calling our desire to us. Our spirit knows no limits and no criticism. It instead craves possibilities for growth and creation. We are at our absolute happiest when we are expressing or expanding our purpose.

As an 8- to 10-year-old child, ideas of how I could make my mark on this vast world were flowing out of me. First I was going to be a vet and help all sick animals. I even opened an animal hospital with my best friend on our street. My allergies proved this to be a difficult road to choose. Undaunted, I decided to be a biologist advocating the importance of wildlife. Still, allergies presented problems. Okay, I'd be a doctor to help people. I was so happy creating, doing, and being the master of my world. Why would I let others tell me who and what I should be? They do not know why I am here on this earth. They do not know my journey.

When I let others dictate what I should do with my life, it was a disaster. I even remember thinking, "This doesn't feel right." However, I listened to my father and not my soul. This led me into marriages that didn't suit me or the life my inner self required. When my energy or soul could not create or expand, it became stuck inside me. I became disconnected from it. At that point in time, what others thought became my guidance. My family, husband, and his family and their ideas were what guided my life.

Our energy/spirit is our being. It is our whole purpose for being on this earth. We are the only ones who know or can learn to know our inner soul. This is our true guidance. It knows what makes us the happiest and our purpose. To listen to others above our own inner selves is to create our own prison.

Sometimes we will be all ready to move forward on our desire when something will stop us in our tracks. Some fear we did not even know we had will appear, causing us to run back into our comfort zone.

One such fear is the fear of success. I first learned about this fear by working with my client, Mark. To tell the truth, I did not even know this fear existed.

Mark was ready to act on his dream. Everything was ready. He even had investors all waiting for him to open his franchise — a building with trampolines for children to jump on in a fairly safe area with supervision. Parents were excited to have a fun place for their children to play and the kids could not wait to jump. Everything was falling into place with ease, yet Mark stopped the process.

"Mark, what is wrong? Why have you decided to put a halt on this awesome dream?" I asked, astounded.

"It is too big! I am amazed with everyone wanting it. It is just too much," he exclaimed, wide- eyed. Finally he said, "What happens if it really takes off?"

This fear of success is very common. As things fall easily into place, this fear takes hold and stops us in our tracks. Understanding that this is what your inner you wants and getting out of its way is necessary. What is really behind this fear of success? Is it not feeling worthy or competent? Is it the feeling of succeeding above your family? Is it feeling you cannot attain things or have achievement in your life? Or is it the fear that life will change?

Patiently looking deep within for the root of the fear and the old, negative paradigms is a way to gently replace this fear with new thoughts of expansion and expression. Although it takes time, it is well worth patience and discovery. Without this fear, you can grow and achieve your dreams.

As Mark repeated his affirmation, "I am strong, capable and able to handle any situation no matter how big or successful it becomes," and kept moving forward on his desire, he found that he could handle the popularity of his trampoline center. He found himself actually having fun.

Everyone has a paradigm that causes them fear to change. With all this fear running around, it is amazing that we accomplish anything.

But what about the people who create lives they love, who make the difference and make the world a better place. Who are these super humans? Surely they are not part of our communities. Maybe they are aliens taking over our world. How do they do it?

Some say it takes being a radical. In fact, this term being a radical is popular right now. Radical make-up, radical life, radical everything. What is a radical? It is a person who doesn't care what others think, always thinks outside of the box, doesn't believe in barriers, and feels no need to prove anything.

Even if you are not a radical, you can still live an amazing life and fulfill your desires. It really takes learning how to deal with these fears. Because you have been working with the "tools" that have helped you to reach outside your situation, you are already on your way. Why? Because you already know to listen to your inner self. You are meditating, practicing gratitude, valuing yourself, surrendering to the universe and believing.

Even with these "tools," these fears can still knock you for a loop. When this happens, do my favorite exercise to feel your spirit. I have a wonderful exercise given to me from a healer and friend.

Go to your favorite place to relax or meditate and allow your mind to slow. Don't get angry with these doubts and fears. Instead, acknowledge that they are there and let them go. Close your eyes and picture your physical self. How beautiful you are. The beauty of your hair, face, hands, and body. Now begin to focus on the small light you have in your abdomen. Ask it to grow and fill your heart. Feel your heart expand and come alive. Allow your energy/spirit to grow so big it expands outside your body in all its glorious light and color. This awesome light does not have any limits. It wants to create and expand. It doesn't care what our mothers say or what the neighbors expect. It doesn't understand why you are stopping yourself with negativity and it knows it can achieve anything it wants because that is its purpose. This is your energy/spirit. It is your light. It is you.

If that all-knowing past, present, and future light doesn't care, why should the physical you?

The limitations, negative thoughts, or social obligations are not us. They are the false us created by others or experiences that left a mark in our lives. Our pure self is our real self. This is the part of us we should and must believe in, listen to, and allow to guide us. Only when we open ourselves to who we really are can we receive all the glorious wonders and abundance of our world.

Take Time to Focus:

1. Find some time to relax and think of what keeps you stuck. Is there a fear or a negative thought that enters your head every time you want to try something new? Write down the comments or fears you find limiting you. Now list three ways you can make your idea happen. This may take a few tries, but be persistent.

2. Go back to chapter 9 on self-esteem and paradigms. Read through the different methods on working through limiting beliefs and give one or more a try. You may use all of them depending on what feels right with each non-serving old belief.

3. Copy and read the affirmation below. Make sure to read it no fewer than three times a day, more if you can. Read it while looking in a mirror covering one eye and then read again covering the other eye.

AFFIRMATION: I, (*insert name*), am master of my ship and captain of my soul. Only I know what my purpose is on this earth. I am strong, capable, and filled with energy of perfection. I will start **today** to make my desire of_____ into my reality.

Date_____

CHAPTER 16
Actions Tell Our Story:

Thought

In order to change your life,
you must change your thoughts;
you must raise your vibration.
It is not only being positive.
It is changing beliefs

How important are our thoughts? How many thoughts do you have during the day? So many it is impossible to count. How many are positive, uplifting, and full of purpose? Or are they negative, pulling you down, or idle chatter? Quantum physics has proven that thoughts are energy. Even more important to us is the fact that they function on vibrations. Our thoughts are powerful. They influence us and the world as we see it. This means what we think about — our happiness or our greatest fear, is actually vibrational energy that affects us in a positive way or brings about the fear we fixate on.

This is why people who say "life is hard" really do experience a hard life. Those who feel everyone around them cheats, often cheat themselves and get cheated on. This is because they are on the vibration of cheating. More of the same will come to them. It is the Law of Attraction and it forms our lives. It is up to us to choose what we want to attract or have in our lives.

My friend Tanya always has a smile on her face and welcomes everyone warmly. She has been through a divorce, but gets along well with her ex, has a great career and children that she loves and adores, and a relationship with a man she describes as wonderful. I have never heard her utter a negative comment, nor have I heard slander or gossip come from her lips. Instead she talks of ideas, possibilities, and you and your interests. Of course she may have an obstacle pop up in her life, but she sees them as obstacles and not problems. Obstacles are something to conquer. Was Tanya born a little optimistic star? No, she knows the power of her thoughts. She has decided how she wants her life to be. She will not think or accept living any other way, nor will she entertain thoughts that bring her out of her vibration. This is a decision.

All strength and weakness, sadness and joy, success and failure is of our own making. All of our happiness and our sorrow are evolved from deep inside us. As we believe, so we become; as we continue to believe and think, so we continue to stay.

We truly are the masters of our conditions and lives. It is time to take responsibility and make them what we want them to be. You are learning more and more about yourself and the type of behavior that helps you create the world you want to live in. Now is the time to feed the positive thoughts and allow them to grow. This is done by constantly seeing yourself respond to any situation the way you know and want to be. It is being focused and persistent on what you want to achieve. It is staying aware to everything wonderful this world has to offer. It is enjoying your journey and blessings in life as you move towards your goal. Negativity will not serve you.

Negativity grows like weeds. Listen to conversations around you. One person will say something negative, then another will respond with another negative comment, and then it builds to take over the whole conversation.

It is like a garden. You carefully plant the beautiful flowers, fertilize and water. Everything is growing nicely and then a weed appears. If that weed is not pulled, another will appear and then another. Soon the whole garden will be overtaken by weeds and will choke out the beautiful flowers you planted.

Negative comments and thoughts are like weeds. They will choke out all your ideas and efforts to make a beautiful life if you do not pull them out. You are the master of the garden. You are the master of your life!

My children laugh, but as they grow they are beginning to understand more why I won't allow the term, "I can't" in our home. If you are busy thinking, "I can't," you are blocking every productive thought in solving the problem. Instead think, "How can I..." which allows for productive thinking. It sounds so simple, and it is, but it is also very important.

Thought and Your Future

Your thoughts can also affect your belief on what you want your future to be. I always think of the children's stor*ies that encourage us to think all was possible.* No matter what the obstacle, or what someone else said to a little engine, or a fair maiden, each would keep saying "I think I can." or "I know it will be." It did not matter what obstacle blocked their way – achieving their goal was a must.

In order to change your life, you must change your thoughts; you must raise your vibration. It is not only being positive. It is changing beliefs. Every day try to improve your thinking, your views, your ideas. Do not allow thoughts that lower vibration, do not serve you, or do not serve your ideas to enter your mind. Strengthen your convictions. Become aware when your vibration doesn't feel good and take action to raise it. Why are you doing what you are doing? Why do you want to achieve what you want to achieve? Have strong, clear views that support these questions. Try, every day, to acquire more views that support these questions.

Why did I write this book? Why do I spend so much time studying, questioning myself and others, and writing? Because my true purpose is to help people who want to have a better life achieve their goal. In order for me to provide that as best I can, I need to keep my mind growing, learning, and developing. I look for ideas and information that will help me attain my purpose. I do not have time for or interest in gossip or "I can't." They do not serve me. They do not help me to achieve my goal. I rejoice in every day and I am very grateful. I look for opportunities, possibilities, and answers that give clearer views to support my desires. I like feeling good, opening my eyes to the possibilities and gifts. I like seeing the good in everyone and I like feeling good about myself. There is no need for negativity because that negates how I want to feel.

If you have found your true purpose or what you really want for your life, really knowing that you will achieve it is imperative. Believing in yourself and all your abilities makes all the difference. Do not allow all the fear and doubt to come into your mind. If you lack confidence, it is time to correct your thoughts. Write on a small card: "I am strong. I can conquer any obstacle. I believe in me." Or if something else resonates with you more, use it. Carry the card in your pocket and read several times a day with feeling. Really let yourself feel strongly about it. Do this until it is constantly in your head.

Vicky loves her life. She has had a fulfilling career as a counselor, raised four beautiful children and has a wonderful husband that she adores. If you ask Vicky how she created this amazing life, she will tell you it is believing in yourself, your desire to change and thinking positively. You will never hear negativity around her. If someone starts to talk negatively, she changes the subject. If a problem is presented, it is presented in a way that it is to be solved. She always sees possibilities and growth and she is not interested in anything stopping or telling her it is not possible.

Your desires and dreams are very special. They are yours. You are the master that can take those desires and dreams and create your reality, your world. No one else can, because they are not you.

It is so important to listen to the inner you and then believe in it with everything you have.

I have stopped counting how many people who have creative, wonderful ideas tell me all the negativity they have to deal with from friends, family and more. They hear constantly that whatever it is they want to achieve is impossible. "How could you even think of doing that?" "I have never heard of such a thing." "Have you ever done that before?" You will find that if you listen to these negative comments it will destroy your belief in yourself, your desire and it will keep you thinking small. It will kill all the flowers in your garden very quickly.

This is why it is important to keep yourself growing, confident, strong and believe in your desires. All the steps you have started to take in this book are to help you keep the positive creativity and love alive. You have been raising your vibration, opening your mind and allowing yourself the freedom to see all possibilities and beauty. You have to foster this and not allow others to tear it down.

Although I tend to be a very optimistic person there are days and people who can bring me down if I allow it. Sometimes the comments aren't even directed at me; however, it is the overwhelming negative feeling of the conversations I hear. Or sometimes I simply get tired and can become negative myself. I have learned to catch this before it happens. No more do I allow myself to endure negative conversations. If I can't change the conversation of the group, then I excuse myself from the group. If I am tired I will put on some uplifting music and meditate or listen and let it lift me. And I certainly will not allow myself to entertain any thoughts that will hurt my self-confidence or my ability to accomplish my desires.

If you feed your mind with negativity, you will see, create and live with negativity. If you feed your mind with the creative, beauty, goodness, love, faith and joy, then your mind opens to all the Universe and its possibilities.

Read books that build your self-confidence. I have already mentioned James Allen's *As a Man Thinketh*. Also, there is a chapter called "Faith" in Napoleon Hill's *Think and Grow Rich*. There is even a formula listed in this chapter to help with self-confidence. Working With the Law by Raymond Holliwell is a wonderful book to understand the Laws of our Universe. There are even wonderful spiritual books that can lift your mind and thoughts.

I understand it takes some effort to watch what we think, say and act. It takes being responsible and owning your own happiness, success, peace, and courage. Likewise, it takes being responsible and owning your own anger, hatred, jealousy, and laziness. No person, place, or event is responsible for your thoughts, actions, and words. You are the master of your life.

Another way I foster shining my light is through meditation. I especially enjoy these when I have been around a lot of negative comments. Here I share some of my favorite meditations:

1. Meditation on joy. All the things in life that bring me joy: my children, my animals, friends, the animal visitors to my yard.
2. Meditation on wonder. The awesomeness of God, the Universe and the beauty of Mother Nature.
3. Meditation on love. Love for my family, my life, and most important, spreading love to every person.
4. Meditation on feeling one with all the life around me. Feeling one with God's universe.

In his book, *As A Man Thinketh,* James Allen says anyone, when left alone, with all going well, can find their goodness and purpose and let it shine. However, when faced with adversity in any form, they will "succumb to hatred, revenge and all-out war."

You, however, are finding your goodness, your purpose, and your true self while facing adversity. You have chosen the higher vibration and for this you should feel great. You have chosen to grow, to have your voice and be who you know you truly are. Be strong and do not let anyone or anything dull your light.

Take Time to Focus:

1. Watch your day. When do you feel drained? Is it after some thing you do, read, listen to? When do you feel alive? What are you doing at that time? How can you increase the alive, vibrant time and decrease the drained time?

2. Write down a short paragraph of your goal or desire. Put it into your pocket. Whenever you feel in doubt read it with conviction.

3. Surround yourself with the positive energy of life. Read books that help you grow, biographies of people you admire, music that lifts your spirit and always open your eyes to the wonder of our world.

AFFIRMATION: I, *(insert name),* will not allow negative thoughts and comments to choke out my desires or my belief in me. I understand if I feed my mind beauty, good- ness, faith, love and joy, I will see with gratefulness my full ability and potential. My dreams and desires deserve to be my realization.

Date: _____

CHAPTER 17

The Power of Imagination:

Visualization

*By visualizing how you will perceive,
respond, and feel in a situation,
you will internalize it and
then act upon it in a way that
causes the situation to change.*

In the chapters on desire, thought, and responsibility, we discuss seeing yourself fulfilling your desire or how you would want to handle a situation. This is called visualization. It is visualizing what you want before it happens.

Daydreaming has been around forever. It wasn't until industry replaced creativity with rote motion that daydreaming was thought to be a waste of time and even dangerous when working machines. In the 1970s, Russian athletes used visualization to help their performance. The athletes would see themselves going through their routines or events in great detail. Many artists, athletes, and other professionals daydream to help them come up with new ideas, further productivity, and solve problems.

Now daydreaming and the use of visualization are seen as beneficial. Even Wikipedia states, "Daydreaming may also help people to sort through problems and achieve success." The newsletter of Pasadena Villa: a Social Integration Model says: "Daydreaming can help relax, manage conflict, maintain relationships and boost productivity."

Many wonderful ideas started as daydreams and moved into visualizations of desires. Without these ideas, daydreams, and visualizations, the light bulb and electricity would not be here. The Wright brothers would not have had the vision to build a flying machine.

So many inventions and life-improving ideas started as dreams and people who believed in their dreams enough to make their dream a desire and make it come true. As I mentioned earlier in the book, Martin Luther King's groundbreaking social justice work all started when he dreamed and visualized a better world.

Our cell phones, TVs, and cars all started as dreams, or actually as ideas that developed into dreams. Next the dream becomes a desire to our minds and details form—so real you feel as if you are already making it happen, step-by-step. Then you are physically acting on your dream. Of course you are. You have already lived every second of it in your mind. You have internalized it! Your dream is now part of you and it is totally natural for you to act upon it.

It is as if you are building a house. You visualize what type of house you would like to live in. You fall in love with your ideal house and start to draw up the plans including every small detail. You then start to build. There you have your house. It is the very same process for creating your life. You have an idea and the more you think about it you make it a desire. You must have this desire, so you start to visualize all the details and make definite plans. The whole time you are sending all this thought energy into the Universe. As you start to act on your plan, you keep your mind on achieving your desire. More and more thought energy reaching the universe. Circumstances and opportunities to help you start to appear and before you know it—you have achieved your desire or purpose.

The inner mind creates your outer reality.

You must realize that this happens with any idea or desire you keep your mind focused on. If you have your mind on anything negative—fear, sickness, or being fired—these will also come true. Your mind and the Universe do not distinguish between the good and the bad. You are in control. Science is discovering more about the abilities of our mind. They are realizing that we have the capacity to heal ourselves much more than ever thought before.

Imagine your perfect life — it's every detail. Now bring that life into your physical reality. It is that simple.

Think of this! You can use this principle of visualization to help situations, relationships, and where you want your life to go.

Too easy? Well, why does something so beneficial to you need to be hard? I have seen people change relationships with their children, mothers, fathers, or business associates. They have changed how others perceive them. I have people tell me that by using visualization, they have made a future situation they were nervous about turn out fine. Others have made their dream future life come into reality.

How can that be? How can they be changing the future? Actually, by visualizing how you will perceive, respond, and feel in a situation, you will internalize it and then act upon it in a way that causes the situation to change.

My son is a very good tennis player. You can often find him sitting quietly with his eyes closed before he plays. At first I thought he was tired, but when I asked what he was doing, he responded, "I am playing tennis." He is visualizing every step. He felt the ball being thrown up for the serve and the power of the racquet as it hits the ball. He sees himself moving and the timing of every return. When he physically starts to play, he is ready in every sense.

Another example: Terry wanted to be a high school English teacher, but was afraid of speaking in public. To be a teacher you must be able to not only speak in public but hold the attention of teenagers from anywhere between one to two hours.

Terry was hired in the spring to start teaching sophomore literature in the fall. She was already nervous and knew she had to conquer this fear of speaking or her desire to teach would vanish. Terry found an excellent speaking coach, with whom she began to meet every week. Next she developed her lesson plans in great detail and then started to visualize teaching the lessons. She saw herself reading, writing on the board, laughing with the kids, and answering their many questions. The more she visualized, the more comfortable she became.

Fall came and Terry was ready. She wasn't as nervous as she thought she might be because she knew this first lesson like the back of her hand. Of course she knew it; she had internalized it.

Walking into the classroom, she barely noticed that there were more students then she had visualized. She started teaching just like she did in her visualizations. When the class was over, Terry was excited. It had gone just like she knew it would.

By Christmas, Terry was one of the most well-liked teachers in the school. The students loved to come and see her even if there wasn't a class. Visualization had helped Terry deal with her fear. This fear was her obstacle and she was not going to accept defeat or failure. She was going to conquer it, and she did!

Visualize something you want to conquer or something you desire. Visualize how it starts and how you want to respond or make it happen. Every detail. Visualize it as often as you can. Try to feel what you would be feeling. Feel the joy when whatever you are visualizing works the way you want it. Notice how you dealt with the situation, how you responded instead of reacting.

When I need to talk to my children about something, I visualize it first. Why? Because when I visualize presenting my concern, I am practicing how I want to appear to them. I do not want to be condescending, angry, or preachy. I do want to ask and listen with an open mind to whatever it is we are discussing at that time. I want to be fair, not judgmental. If I feel I need to teach them something about the situation, I want to stay open and have compassion. So I will visualize the entire discussion a few times until I have internalized it. Every discussion has worked like a dream. Now I really do not need to visualize, because discussing things in this way has become my way.

How we perceive the world is largely due to how we perceive ourselves. If we feel like a victim, we see the world doing things to us.

Thus if we believe in ourselves and like ourselves, we see the love and beauty around us. We can see the world as a beautiful place, full of opportunities for us to explore.

People always say that I am an optimist. Maybe I am. But I feel it has more to do with simply opening my eyes to the wonder before me. I know who I am and I know my strengths. I like myself! And I can't wait to explore this wonderful world every day.

Throughout this book we have explored who we are, what we want to be, and what we want to achieve. We have looked at our strengths, our beauty, and our mistakes. We have forgiven our mistakes and mistakes made by others. We want what is best for all. Now it is time to visualize how to deal with any situation that we are not happy with, or to visualize our desires and how we want to gain them.

I have wanted to write. I wasn't sure what I wanted to write about. I just knew I wanted to write. I also wanted to be home more, to work in a calm, peaceful place instead of running around like I always seemed to be. So I started to visualize myself at home writing—where would I sit, how calm it would be and how happy I would be coming up with a wonderful book. Once I achieved this, I started to visualize how I was going to get this book out to every- one who wanted to read it and learn how to move forward with confidence and purpose into their own bright and shining future.

In the morning right after I list what I am very grateful for, I sit quietly and visualize what I will be doing that day, what I want to achieve and how I will go about achieving it. If I am taking my children to the park, what am I trying to achieve? Well, I want us to have fun, get closer as a family, and enjoy each other. I come up with some games and a picnic lunch, then internalize this picture and this feeling and begin my day.

Throughout my long divorce, I had to go to court several times. I do not like going to court at all, and I despise being put on the stand and asked questions. In the beginning, I would get very nervous weeks before I took the stand. However, once I learned about visualization, my view changed. What did I have to lose? For two weeks before I would be on the stand, I visualized how I wanted to present myself in court. How calm I would be. How I would wait and really think before answering any questions and nothing would ruffle my feathers. I wanted to be seen as strong, capable, and focused on what the issue was for this court session. When the time came, I was amazed how short my time on the stand was. Were the questions easier and more straightforward? Did they not want to know very much? No, that was not it. Actually, I listened calmly and answered without rattling on so it was harder for the opposing attorney to try and trip me up. I still would not say that I enjoy court. However, I am not afraid of going to court anymore. I know I can handle it. Visualization helped me conquer my fear.

Visualization helps many, many people in their lives. There are people who even say it got them out of poverty or gave them the success they wanted in their life. To this I say, of course it did.

Elizabeth needed money. She was newly divorced and on her own with four small children and their father nowhere in sight. Elizabeth had already been working on forgiveness, gratitude, and learning about herself. She had not started to discover her purpose or what she truly desired other than money.

I suggested she write down, "I am happy and grateful for the sum of _____ given to me intermittently through- out the year in exchange for the services I render to the best of my ability as_____." At first she laughed. But when she read it, she said, "Well, I would love to start a landscaping business." So we filled in the blanks with the amount she would like to have at the end of the year and the services she would render as owner of a landscaping business. We made a little card for her to keep in her pocket. Elizabeth was going to read this card every morning and every night along with as many times as she liked during the day.

I also asked her to start visualizing her business down to the smallest detail; how wonderful it felt to receive the money. She was to visualize until she felt like she was already a successful landscaper with a thriving, growing business.

At first she asked how she could get started with her new business. I told her not to worry yet. Everything would present itself when she was ready.

In one month Elizabeth had her first client. She borrowed a truck, used her own tools, and went to work. Her client was so pleased with the results she asked Elizabeth if she would help design a certain area in her yard. Elizabeth gladly accepted. That design launched her career. Now she has three crews that take care of her growing lawn care business. Elizabeth is very busy designing and installing people's beautiful landscapes.

She did have to make a new card, because she doubled what she had thought she would be making in a year.

Why does visualization work? In *Think and Grow Rich,* Napoleon Hill wrote, "Desire is a thought impulse! Thought impulses are forms of energy. When you begin with the thought impulse desire to accumulate money, you are drafting into your service the same "stuff" that nature used in creating this earth and every material form in the universe, including the body and brain in which the thought impulses function." Thought is energy. So when you think a thought, especially over and over, you are sending energy out.

We see the miracle of our world in every plant, building, ocean, mountain, and every little cell that makes us who we are. Every idea and every solution is in the Universe as energy waiting for us to hear. It is amazing. When Elizabeth read over her affirmation and focused her visualizations intently on her definite plan, she was sending out constant thought impulses in the form of energy. By doing this you have "definitely given concrete form to the intangible desire," according to Hill. You are taking the steps to bringing your desire into the "physical equivalent," into your reality and your world.

If you are constantly putting out negative thought impulses, they become the desire and you bring those into the physical equivalent also. That is why our thoughts are so important. What we think, we become or manifest. Anger loves to feed anger. The more anger we feel, the more comes to us and feeds our anger. The more imprisoned, hurt, lost, or confused you feel, the more you bring to you and into physical reality.

Clear your head of all the negative thoughts. Allow yourself to forgive. Be grateful and meditate. These are the tools that help you step through the door and away from your prison. You have already opened the door and started to walk through to a bright, miraculous world. Now it is time to make your desire your new life. Its physical equivalent is only a few thought impulses away.

Once we have our desire and visualize this desire in its completion,
we then want to start taking the steps to get to our goal.
Often when we desire to achieve our goal,
we start with a definite plan.
You are now on your way to manifesting your life.

Take Time to Focus:

1. Start your visualization. Begin and relax, breathing deep. Close your eyes and begin to visualize your desire, situations you want to fix, an area in your life that is a problem or a fear that you wish to conquer. Visualize every detail and internalize how it makes you feel. Do this often or at least three times a day to start.

2. Start to act on your visualization. Bring it to your present and don't look back.

3. If you have trouble visualizing your goal focus on the feeling you want to have when you achieve this goal/desire. Gain the feeling first through music or something that makes you happy then picture you attaining your desire.

4. Another way to help further your visualization is using a vision board. Paste or tape on your board pictures that represent your desire, feelings you will have when you achieve your desire and how will attaining this desire change your life for the better? Hang your vision where you can see it often. Allow yourself to feel the happiness and satisfaction you will feel when you attain you goal

AFFIRMATION: I,_(*insert name*)_ am acting on my visualizations. I focus on my future and what I want it to be. I do not look back. All beauty, goodness, love, hope and joy are present in me. I am free to make my life what I want it to be.

Date: _____

CHAPTER 18

Ah! The Freedom:

Letting Go!

Instead trust the inner part of you.
This inner divine energy of you is your guide.
Believe in yourself and trust your desire will be fulfilled.

But what if I am unsure of how to obtain my goal? What if I have no idea how to obtain what I need to achieve my desire?

Let me assure you, this is normal when we are creating something new, different and life changing. What do you think Steve Jobs, Henry Ford, or Edison did with these magnificent and seemingly unreachable goals? They kept the vision clear in their mind, had the faith it would be so and they began walking towards it with persistence even though the path they traveled was uncharted.

When I decided I wanted my first book, "You Can't Escape from a Prison if You Don't Know You're In One: What is Blocking Your Freedom?" to be a bestseller, I had no idea how to make it happen. I had never written a book let alone sell a book I have written to thousands of people. How was I going to get my book to all these people? I had no idea, but I did have faith that I would be a bestselling author. I did have a starting plan of telling everyone I knew or met to read my book. Every seminar, workshop, coffee shop I attended, people would know who I am and have a way to buy my book.

If you firmly believe, completely internalize your desire then something magical happens. The Universe says, "Okay Alena, you want to be a bestselling author? We will help but you have to keep your eyes open and take the opportunities."

So even though I knew what I wanted to achieve, how to start to proceed and the persistence to keep walking forward, becoming my desire, I kept my eyes open to opportunities. Magazines that I did not even realize knew who I was asked me to write an article. Other authors and bloggers allowed me to write for their blogs. Every opportunity which appeared to help me attain my goal I gladly received. I trusted people who had attained this type of goal before or something just as important.

What I learned through my bestseller journey was to let go of the "how" and to walk the journey but not get caught up in every step. Keep your faith, walk towards your goal and let go of the "how".

Many get caught up in everything happening the way they want it to happen. They create a definite plan however they get stuck in the little things and close their eyes to opportunities. When a mistake is made or things do not end up as was the plan, they will often give up on their dream. "It just wasn't working out" or "It isn't meant to be" are common terms we tell ourselves.

Instead, trust the inner part of you. This inner divine energy of you is your guide. Believe in yourself and trust your desire will be fulfilled. If you have questions, then surround yourself with people who have answers. Even with their knowing you must first trust your inner self. When you trust this guidance from inside you change the whole journey. Mistakes are lessons to learn and move forward wiser. It never enters you mind to stop or that things "aren't working out." It is a learning and evolving journey in becoming your desire. There will be mistakes and there will be times when you make leaps and bounds – a quantum leap! But it is still all part of the journey of you.

Say I desired to be the perfect mom to my three children. I do not think being the best mom I can be is enough. I have set the goal for being the perfect mom. I come up with my plan of how I want to attain my goal. If I start acting my plan with faith that I will be the perfect mom – surrender my goal to the Universe -- then I allow myself to stay open to better methods or insight, grow from mistakes and think from my mind and heart. I gain an inner knowing that I will be the mom I want to be. The thoughts and feelings of my children would be of major importance and we would grow and learn together. This allows the process of becoming the perfect mom to happen in the best way for all.

If, however, I start acting on my plan thinking, "I have to be the perfect mom. Every step counts" I have created an ego pressure to achieve the goal for myself. I have to do it. There is no room for mistakes because I have to be the perfect mom – I have to attain my goal. It is all about me and only me – the ego. I am not thinking that what I want has to do with anyone else but me. The natural process of growth and faith are removed and only the ego is identifying with "I will be the perfect mom." When I make a mistake, I take it personally. "How could I be so stupid? I am not the perfect mom." Then my desire dies.

Letting go of the "how" and instead having faith allows us the freedom for flexibility and gaining inner knowing that yes, I am attaining my goal. When we get hung up on the "how" or the steps instead of letting go we create a wall between what we think it should be and what the Universe is providing to help us grow and attain the desire. This is important. Never have any of my so-called achievements in life come from how I planned it. An opportunity seemed to just appear or the situation would suddenly change that would help me.

Letting go is keeping our goal in site but surrendering the "how" to the universe or God. We remain open to experiment, make mistakes and learn knowing that somehow we will reach our goal.

An excellent example is my friend Ron. Ron wanted to paint landscapes and houses. He wanted to "bring the world to life through art". Even before he started to seriously paint Ron would say to himself and others, "My work as an artist will change the concept of art." Ron had no idea how he was going to achieve this goal. He did not identify with what he thought an artist who changes the concept of art would be. He simply kept the faith that it was going to happen and allowed himself to be guided.

When Ron started to paint he found that there was nothing special about his pictures – something was missing. He would often quietly stare at his painting and then back at the landscape he was painting. Never did I see him get upset or worried that he was not achieving the uniqueness he was seeking. Instead he patiently painted trying different perspectives, angles or shading. Allowing the scene and painting guide him to a new perspective.

Ron was letting go and actually enjoying the discovery of his work. He enjoyed trying new techniques or changing the perception of the landscape. Even with all his trial and error, he would still say, "I am bringing my picture to life." If he made a mistake, he would shake his head and wipe the canvas clean.

Ron had developed a firm and deep knowing that what he wanted to achieve would definitely happen. He had total faith and trusted his inner self to guide him, and he let go of trying to guess how it was going to happen. He did not go through the process thinking he knew what was best instead he let go and allowed his work to unfold to him.

It was this letting go that actually opened his mind to playing with the light in a new and different way in his paintings. How he chose to portray the light changed the meaning of the painting – brought it to life. Soon all the area galleries wanted to display his paintings. People were amazed with the beauty and the interesting perspective Ron offered with his play on the light.

Now Ron is beginning to see what he knew all along. His art was coming to life and the Universe brought him even more because people loved his work. His work was becoming popular.

Ron's ability to let go of the process allowed him to be set free to find the very thing that made him well known for his art.

If you are working on achieving your purpose or desire, first internalize your worthy goal. It becomes a deep knowing that it will happen. Allow it to become a belief of your desire and in your inner knowing – it simply will be. Second, let go of the "how" or process. We don't always know how our desire will appear. Many times it is not as we planned. I never thought that by losing the court battle I would not only win what was best for my children, but also what was best for the whole family.

Letting go allows you to explore. Sure you may have temporary defeat, but remember, it is temporary. Learn and grow from it, then try a different route. Ron experimented, contemplated and studied his art. Mistakes were learned from then wiped away to try something different. It was this daring to be different and not being afraid of defeat that allowed Ron to discover his success.

It must be noted that every person who finds success has had some temporary defeat along the way. It is how we deal with this defeat that makes us a success. If we allow it to stop us and end our desire, then we are done. If we instead learn from it, we can let it go or move on to something better. Our desires and dreams are much too precious to give up. Mistakes and setbacks are obstacles to learn from, not to stop the process. In fact, they are part of the process of becoming. Learn from them, let them go and move on to something even better.

Letting go of a process is living in the focused present, walking towards our desire with action, making the best decisions we can and most importantly, learning, and enjoying the ride.

Holding on to the pain

Letting go or surrendering the "how" is one way of letting go while attaining our purpose or desire. Another letting go has to do with the past. Regret, hurt, anger all put chains on our heart and many can forgive the person but still hold on to the pain. There is an old saying, "an elephant never forgets." Now I do not know if this is true, however the saying means, forgive but don't forget. And yes, in one way we do not forget. We should harvest the lesson that allows us to grow in a positive way, not close us off or continue to feel isolated.

We can sometimes identify with the hurt or anger more than with the actual person or circumstance that caused the hurt. We think we have forgiven but still hold on to the anger or hurt in our heart.

Now that I am single and have worked with so many after divorce, I see how people hold on to the pain. They have trouble trusting another person. This is a chain around their heart. If you do not feel that you can trust, you can never open your heart totally to a person who may love you with their whole heart.

The anger or hurt can affect us in other areas of our life. I learned this when I worked with Tony.

Recently I met with Tony for coffee. Tony had a rare condition that caused him to lose a full scholarship at a university and a career in the armed forces. Throughout his life this rare health condition seemed to prohibit him from attaining the life he wanted to live. Tony had Addison's disease. This is when the body does not make the cortisone it needs to survive. Every day Tony needed to take cortisone, if he missed than he would go into a coma and possibly die. Although Tony had come to terms with his condition and the realization of his career limitations, he still felt angry. He didn't understand it, but he found it showed in how he looked at everyday life and how people reacted to him. Tony wanted to learn how to let go of the deep anger he knew he felt but did not understand why.

Each step Tony took to let go of the deep anger showed him the benefit of letting go. His body began to relax. The pain in his shoulders went away. Meditation brought a calmness to his mind and heart. With gratefulness he found himself smiling and laughing more. Each tool helped to break the hold anger had on him – he was gaining freedom.

The big break for Tony came one day in a meditation when the reason for his anger sprang to his consciousness. He was not angry at his own condition, but at others who did not understand it and put limitations upon him. He did not like the special treatment, sympathy and the "You can't do this or that" he heard from people. It made him feel helpless, like a victim. Now that Tony understood why he felt the anger he could start the process of letting go. He could release the feeling of anger once he came to the awareness that he did not have to feel like a victim. He could control the way he felt even if others did not understand.

Tony began to practice meditation regularly. After he was comfortable with just being, he began to visit his anger. He spoke to the anger and the situation he often faced with others. Slowly, as he invited the new control over the situation to enter, he was able to say goodbye to this long held friend. Anger left and Tony was now in control of how he wanted to feel and deal with his life.

Tony felt a new sense freedom. He became happier and as his happiness grew he noticed how people reacted happier towards him. He found he could talk to people on a deeper level. People soon started to ask him more and more questions about what he was learning. He found himself enjoying helping others learn and better their lives. Now he has made this his life purpose. Tony helps people let go of the pain or hurt and live happier, fuller lives. He harbors no anger about his own health, instead he believes he has his condition to help others understand their pain.

Many people are very good at pushing their feeling way down inside them. The problem is that these feelings do not go away. Instead they reveal themselves in subtle ways that affect how we see ourselves, our lives and the people around us.

The first course of action is acknowledging that you feel the anger, hurt or pain. I remember my frustration came out in conversations or just popped into my head. I coined these incidents "popcorn" because they just seemed to pop out of me.

It wasn't until I accepted that yes, I did feel frustrated, that I could reach inside myself and explore the "why" through a gentle meditation and spirit writing.

Spirit writing/conscious writing is a wonderful way to find answers to what ails you. First find a comfortable place and relax with a paper and pen close by. When you feel open and relaxed write your intention at the top of the paper. Mine was "Why am I feeling so frustrated?" Then begin to write. At first the writing may feel very logical and conscious. Keep writing! Soon you will open to a deeper part within you. Feelings, emotions and memories will start to emerge.

Once you know why you're feeling the way you do, you can forgive, heal and let go.

Nothing is more physically or emotionally freeing than letting go of a negative emotion you have been holding deep within yourself. You owe it to yourself, your future and those you love to let go and open yourself to life.

The choices we make while leaving our prison can affect how easily we let go!

Hopefully by now you can see how holding on to negative feelings can hurt you physically, those around you and hold you back from living a life you want to live.

Those who are leaving a very difficult prison or situation are probably starting to let go as you forgive and harbor no ill. You let go more if you feel you have done everything in your power to make sure your choices were as beneficial to all as possible. The outcome is not always under your control. Let go! You have meditated and looked inside to find the special person you truly are, a person with compassion and joy. You are grateful for so many gifts in your life. You have been taking responsibility for you, knowing you are the creator of your destiny, the master of your ship, not anyone else or any situation—only you! You are letting go! You feel your own strength and know you have a purpose. You will be who you are meant to be. You will shine your own light. Let go!

If you are in an arduous situation, letting go is essential. You want things to turn out the way you imagine. But you can't hold onto things you can't control. Be true to who you are, do your best to be fair with all and hand it up to The Universe, or God. Let it be the process. A long, arduous prison can wear you down and leave you with a lot of anger and regret. It can create a vicious, vengeful cycle that can go on for years. This can hurt the family more than you know and it will keep you in that awful, vengeful place.

When I met Katrina she was in her fourth year of her divorce. Although she wanted very much to end her marriage and the difficult divorce, her soon-to-be-ex did not feel the same. He found delight in tormenting and prolonging the process.

Katrina began to work with me. She practiced the tools of awareness, gratitude, acceptance, surrender but stopped at forgiveness and letting go. The length and hurt of her divorce seemed so alive to Katrina. She just could not forgive. Without the forgiveness, it is impossible to let go. So Katrina continued to hold on to the feelings of frustration, hurt and anger until finally, one month later she was able to objectively view her marriage and what had caused the divorce to continue in such a long and hurtful way.

That was the point Katrina understood her part in the story. She began to see how one event led to another; how the attorneys were also trying to continue the fight. The pieces of the puzzle were becoming clear to Katrina. She was now able to see above the trees of the forest. She could now rise above all the hurt and anger to see the situation for what it was along with what would be best for everyone concerned.

Katrina was then able to forgive and let go. This new awareness gave her confidence and new strength. She understood and knew how to end the divorce in the best way possible. Two months later Katrina was a happily divorced woman, ready to move on with her life.

This is why I wrote the book. I wrote it for people going through these nightmare situations. You are not alone and you can, more than ever, rise above it all and come out with your purpose and definitely your confidence, ready to move on into your awesome life. Letting go is the key.

The bars that hold you so firmly in place are of your own making. You alone have the key to your freedom.

I have a secret to share, though you might already have figured it out: The prison that has held you, your prison, is self-made.

How does it feel to read the above statement? Are you surprised, or do you say, "Of course it is"? Are you making a list of alibis?

Prisons are self-made because we are the master of our fates. As you have been learning throughout this book, you are in control of your thoughts, vibration, self-image, desires and you. No one else is in control of you. If you are in a prison, you have put yourself there. Of course it was without your knowledge at the time. Now you have the knowledge. You see clearly all the endless possibilities and how very big we really are. With that knowledge alone, there is no use for prisons. The only one keeping you there is you.

Step out of your prison. Walk through the door to your future. There is absolutely no reason to hang onto anything that brought you unhappiness or pain. Learn the lesson, leave the rest behind and move forward.

What does Deepak Chopra mean when he says "you will lose many things from the past"? Well, it means you have to let go of all the stuff you don't need anymore. The one important fact to remember is that the past is just that, the past. The moment in time is gone. You cannot change what happened and it doesn't serve you to relive the past over and over with feelings of anger or hurt. Letting go allows you to find the true you or "permanent self." It is the part of you that is ever expansion and expression. As Deepak says so eloquently, "Once you capture this you have captured the world."

That "stuff" doesn't define who you are becoming or want to become, and the situations associated with the "stuff" don't move you in the direction you want and need to go.

You now have your desire and definite plan to create the life you are meant to live. Let go of things that do not serve your purpose and your desire. Let go of old habits, situations, and yes, even friends who are not helping you attain your goal.

Lucy had her desire and her plan. She was leaving her job as hairdresser and going back to school to learn to be a chef. Everything financially was working out; however, some hair clients didn't want her to leave, so she agreed to keep doing their hair. In the beginning her friends and family thought she was crazy for going back to school, then they were excited for her.

Lucy started school and soon became very busy. There was so much to learn and the work could become overwhelming at times. Lucy was having a hard time living in two worlds. Long hours at school left very little time to get back to the salon and do hair. Her clients were becoming tired of her being late. She had her schoolwork, friends from school and she had her friends from her previous work. The more involved with school she became, the more resentful her friends from her hairstyling days became until they decided she didn't have anything in common with them anymore. They let her go.

At first Lucy was very upset. After really looking at what she wanted to achieve and how it had weighed her down to hold onto what was in her past and no longer served her, she too let go.

Only you know what you need to do. Sometimes we are talked into holding on by friends, family, or the situation itself. Or sometimes we are simply afraid to let go. Hopefully you have learned there is absolutely nothing to be scared of and everything to rejoice in.

So many when it is time to leave this earth feel regret. Never have I heard people say they regret what they have done in life. No, it is the dreams, hopes and desires they did not fulfill or even try to achieve. It is becoming the dancer, author, singer or doctor, scientist that our hearts cried for us to be. It is the unresolved hurt in once very close relationships. These are the regrets people die with in their hearts.

When asked why they did not fulfill their own wishes, they answer with limitations. Either they blame family obligations, social acceptance or expectations, not able to believe it was possible or just too caught up in what others thought of them. Learning that our true self is so much bigger than any of these limitations is the beginning to the end of regret.

Allow yourself freedom. Allow yourself the ability to build your future. Allow yourself to be happy with who you are and what you can do. Allow yourself peace! Allow yourself to build on positive motions forward in your relationships and life choices. The only way is to first let go of anything that does not serve our growth as a person and as the true energy/ spirit we are. Why delay?

No matter what it is surrender and let it go! What you will gain is faith in yourself, your life and in Divine Source. Faith of who you want to be and what you want to achieve will fill your heart. This faith and vision will help you step forward with confidence and strength into your future. And why shouldn't it? You are the master of your fate.

Take Time to Focus:

1. What is your desire? What is it that you really want to achieve in your life? First define it. Why do you want it? This is the important question. This question provides you with the bigger picture or looking from above the trees.

2. Write out Why you want to attain this goal and hang it where you can see it all the time. Everytime the details get to be too much or challenges arise – this will help you keep your mission clear.

3. Surrender what you want to the universe. This means visualize it and keep the feeling alive in your heart. Once you do this allow yourself to have the inner knowing that it will be done – Faith! Repeat this step as needed.

4. Develop your plan of action. What steps do you think will help you attain your goal. Start on these steps but let go of the "How". This means stay open, having faith that your goal will be attained and don't be surprised if you achieve it in a different way than you planned.

AFFIRMATION: I, _(insert name)_, let go of all that does not serve me anymore. The past is the past. I let go of the anger, hurt, embarrassment or any other feelings that do not allow me to grow. I am FREE!

Date_____

Welcome to Your Future!

CHAPTER 19

The Road Lies Before You:

The Journey

*Every person who has lived a life they loved
always says it was the journey, the climb.
Each obstacle they conquered
or achievement they achieved by growing was
the joy of their life.*

There you have it! These are the "tools" the Universe provided to help me break free and transcend a very difficult four and a half-year divorce. Every lesson/tool came to me at just the right time, sometimes in ways I wasn't even sure were good. The key was to always keep my eyes open and thankful. Jesus said "eyes of a child." He really meant open without doubt, judgment or criticism but instead filled with gratefulness and wonder. It is looking with the eyes of our inner selves. We simply have to get out of our own way. Then the way becomes clear.

To this day I still feel that it was because I had forgiven, harbored no ill will towards my ex-husband and his family, that when I lost the child support in court, I still received what I needed for my children's college education. Even during the court proceedings I forgave everything. I decided to let go of the whole process and begin to move on with my future and purpose. Actually, when I found out I had lost the appeal, I wasn't even upset. I had surrendered the process and the result, asking for "the betterment of all." So my losing, I figured, was for the betterment of all.

Later that month I received a call from my ex-husband's family explaining to me that they understood what I was wanting and not to worry because it would all be taken care of at the appropriate time. I was astounded. The Universe/God did give me "the betterment of all." Now there were no hard feelings for either side. Instead, we were helping each other and the children.

It truly is wanting your desire/purpose, having the unshakable faith that it will be so and surrendering the "how" and maybe sometimes the result to "the betterment of all involved" that manifests OUR dreams into reality.

You, too, have learned to let go during the process; now allow all the work you have done on yourself to pay off. Now you can see clearly all aspects of the situation and where you want to be. You feel strong and confident and you know yourself. It is time to leave anything you do not need behind and move into your future.

I am very excited for you. Now that you have started this journey of discovery of you, continue. This is an ever-evolving process. Continue to discover and grow. Life truly gets better and better!

Are you finished with the "tools" once you begin to live the life you love? Absolutely not. These tools grow as you evolve. It is incredibly easy, as life becomes busy, to forget to practice the tools.

When life is going well, our vibration is high and we feel good. Many times we put aside writing out the gratitude, meditating, or taking time for ourselves. It is easy to be in a high vibration when life is going well. When an obstacle or challenge enters our world, we are unprepared and wonder what happened. Sometimes there isn't even an obstacle. We just feel bogged down in the everyday hustle and bustle of it all. We wonder what is missing. Why did we feel so alive before? It is because we have become disconnected from our inner self again.

Dalton finally had the car dealership he wanted. The cars were selling well and the dealership was constantly growing. Dalton was busy trying to build the business, train and keep employees happy, and satisfy the customers. There never seemed to be enough hours in a day, but Dalton didn't mind. He loved the business — it was his dream come true.

Once the business started to plateau, the excitement settled down a little, Dalton started to feel a little bothered. He couldn't put his finger on the reason why, but he was becoming a little nervous and unsatisfied. Little things began to bother him. Life seemed to have lost is magic.

Dalton was relying on the situation or circumstance to raise his vibration. He was building his dream, and the excitement of seeing his dream come alive made him feel alive. But when the excitement of the situation settled down, so did Dalton.

It is very easy to feel alive when everything is going our way. This is letting the outside circumstances determine our happiness. We are not starting with the happiness inside ourselves. This happens through growth of our spirit or inner energy. Meditation, reading/studying, gratitude, and connecting with our inner self all create the feelings from within us. When we forget ourselves we start to rely on outside forces to dictate our feeling.

It is vitally important to keep growing inside.

So much has happened since I broke free from my personal prison. I am now an international bestselling author and speaker, and I mentor many on breaking free and living a life they love. Launching programs, teaching classes, and interviewing for the podcast show all take time. Sometimes it can feel a little overwhelming if I am not connected to my higher self.

Every morning I write out my gratitude list, ask for guidance and send blessing to those who may be bothering me. I study by reading authors that teach me more about myself. During the day I raise my vibration with music, a walk in nature, dancing, or writing. In the afternoon I make sure to meditate and take time for myself. I am always feeding my soul and growing in my ideas and new beliefs.

Each day feels like a blessing. No matter what is going on around me, I see and feel the wonder of our universe. Challenges or mistakes do happen; however, they don't affect me very much. I look for new ways to solve a problem, learn what I need, and let go.

We are amazing creatures. We can achieve anything we set our minds on. We are the highest form of creation and have Infinite Source flowing through us. We owe it to ourselves to be responsible for the growth of the inner part of us. To keep the channels open and free so the energy can flow freely through us.

Sometimes life gets so good we begin to take advantage of those sent to help us.

It's funny how simple the concept is and yet so many people let it go when they think they can do everything by themselves. First, no one does anything by themselves. The Universe sent me experiences and mentors in every step of my growth. I could have said, "No thank you.

I got this." Instead I took the opportunities given to me. These mentors all had information and lessons for me. If I had decided not to take the opportunity, I would have missed the lesson. Some of these lessons were huge — being a victim is a choice; forgiveness and letting go set us free, and we are the masters of our fate and the captains of our souls. Finally, when I taught hundreds through the court system, I learned that these tools are for everyone. Lives are changed for the better and people are happier. These are the reasons I published this book.

Just recently I met with my mentor and he asked, "Is your program done?"

I replied, "No because we are having problems getting Infusion Soft loaded on the computer."

He asked again, "Why isn't your program done?"

And I replied again, "We are having problems loading up the computer program"

This went on for what seemed to be three minutes. All of a sudden I got it. Why was the difficulty loading a program on the computer causing me to not write a self-help program to help the people? I was letting my circumstances dictate what I was able to accomplish. We both received a good laugh from my slight stubbornness in learning this lesson. Now we have a running joke. When I handed him my program, "Breaking Free," I told him he deserved the first copy because he had to hit me over the head six times before I learned the lesson.

However, there was another lesson in this interaction with my mentor: Patience and allowing the person to discover. If he had simply said, "It doesn't matter if the program is working on the computer. You can still do your work," it would not have hit home as strongly as when I come to the discovery myself. He chose to guide me into the discovery.

Both these lessons I might not have learned on my own. The Universe brings us people and events to help us evolve. It is up to us to choose whether we accept these gifts or ignore them. Neither way is wrong; it is like choosing a road to travel. The road can be more direct and easier or have many turns and obstacles. It is up to the traveler to choose which road they like to travel.

There is always more to learn because your soul/energy is evolving, and this naturally brings new challenge. How we choose to handle these challenges can lead to our inner self growth and wisdom.

Working with people as my mentors worked with me, I have learned incredible stories and amazing victories. If I can get people to tap into their inner strength, they can move mountains. I can see in every person the goodness, vibrancy, and joy inside them. And through my continual inner growth and study, I have the peace within myself and the knowledge to help others bring forth the goodness and vibrancy from within themselves.

The Sneaky Ego

You, too will see how you are treating every aspect of your life, every situation, every person or relationship differently. You will find yourself being observant, open, compassionate, slow to judge, and accepting. You will know when to respond to a situation and when doing so will not serve you. And because you continue to be grateful, you will always see the glory, beauty, and goodness of this life of yours.

Patience with yourself and your growth is the key. Sometimes we get off track. Planes traveling from one point to another will get off track hundreds of times. Each time they are guided by an inner system to get right back on track. The same goes for us. We will get off the track as life gets busy or we feel we can do it alone, but if we have been keeping connected to our inner self, we will notice when we don't feel right. The magic is gone or life has lost its sparkle. We simply have to unblock and open up our connection and we are back on track.

The ego can sometimes grow and everything becomes "I". "Only I can do this." "It's my dream." "It's my ability that makes everything happen."

Vernon Howard in his book, *The Mystic Path to Cosmic Power*, speaks about the false self and the true self. Ego is our false self. It is the self full of negativity and solitude. The "I" becomes the only important being. Everything will be done to protect it.

The true self is what we have learned in this book, our inner self. It is one of freedom, connection, understanding, and knowing. It is the part of us that opens all blocks to create free energy or soul. Our inner self, true self is the self of expansion and expression while the ego is the self of protection, fear, and doubt.

If you find ego sneaking back into your thinking, don't fret. Have patience with yourself. Remember the plane getting itself back on course with its inner system. By using the tools, you can get yourself back on course with your inner guidance. You have got this.

It is funny, but the more I live and love my life, the more I thank Source/God for the experiences that helped me get here, including my marriage and divorce. Without losing my love for life and experiencing what happens when we let others choose our lives, I would never value my freedom and who I am as much as I do now. I would never understand how to help others achieve their freedom and love for living. I probably would not have opened myself to the discovery of my inner self.

It is this experience of losing myself and my life that allowed me to love my life again. It was my wake-up call.

Life is precious. We have such a short time on this earth to create everything we came here to create. Why waste the time we have on silly negativity, blaming, or allowing others to control our lives? It is so much more fun to feel in control of ourselves, know ourselves, and feel the support and love of this Infinite Source.

Choosing to live our lives from our highest perspective is opening the door to our glorious true selves. It is then that our lives become magical. It is your life and it is meant to be lived the way you want to live it. You are blooming and growing and, most importantly, believing in yourself.

Every person who has lived a life they loved always says it was the journey, the climb. Each obstacle they conquered or achievement they achieved by growing was the joy of their life. Not once did I hear someone say, "Wow, I am so happy I played it safe even if I didn't do anything great; I was safe." Instead, it is the joy of discovery, trusting in themselves and in something bigger and going with everything they had, to accomplish what they believed could be. This is what we are here on this glorious planet to do – the incredible, sometimes difficult, but always rewarding journey!

You are ready to begin you journey. Enjoy this awesome life you are creating. Shine that special light of yours that only you can shine!

Live Free! Let Go

Take Time to Focus:

1. Continue to write in your notebook. Write any quotes you love or questions you want to meditate on. If you are having any doubt, write on it, meditate and come up with answers. Work on deepening your desire and having faith and confidence in yourself and your ideas.

2. Read the book Think and Grow Rich by Napoleon Hill. It is a wonderful book that will continue to help you on your ever-evolving journey.

3. Always be grateful.

> *Sing like no one is listening,*
> *Love like you've never been hurt,*
> *dance like nobody is watching,*
> *and live like it's heaven on earth.*
> **—MARK TWAIN**

YOUR NEXT STEPS...

Grab Some Free Gifts, Get Ongoing Support, And More!

Congratulations!

You've made it to "The Back of The Book" – and I sincerely hope you've found what you need, between these covers.

I've certainly tried to pack as much as possible into this book – the most powerful strategies and techniques I know to cope with Life's many tragedies and setbacks, and then transform YOUR life into one you can LOVE.

Let's keep the conversation going...

Now I would like to invite you to visit my website at www.alenachapmanlife.com

There, you can claim a special FREE GIFT I've set aside just for you. And when you do...

You can also take advantage of a FREE subscription to my "Prison Break" email updates – tips and strategies that extend the power of what you've already learned here, mailed straight to your Inbox. (It's not a regularly-scheduled thing, and I will never "overwhelm" you with emails.)

And check out my Blog while you're there! Read through a few posts to get a feel for what's in store EVERY time you visit. (I recommend you bookmark the site, too, so you can easily get back any time you want to.)

My website is the perfect way to keep this conversation going, and offers you so many options to get the additional help you might need – solutions and guidance you won't find anywhere else!

Like my collection of guided and non-guided **"Meditations"** audios – exclusively crafted to help you...

- Live a life of **abundance**, attracting and manifesting ALL the things you desire and deserve. (Not just "possessions" and achievements but love, confidence, contentment, and more!)
- Fill your heart with **forgiveness** – for others AND for yourself.
- Achieve a sense of **oneness** with not only friends and family ... but also with yourself, your Creator, and the world around you.
- Master the art of **visualization** – so you can see, feel, smell, taste, and hear those things you wish to attract into, or changes you want to bring about in, your life.

Each of these meditations, by itself, is powerful enough to effect tremendous change in your life by reshaping your beliefs and behavior. But as a set, their transformative power is MULTIPLIED – boosting your enjoyment of ALL areas of Life.

And if you would like even MORE help...

Listen, we can all use a little more help, sometimes.

That's why I've created several training and coaching programs that guide you to recovery and transformation in a variety of ways – for those people with grander goals, or who need more help than I can provide in this book or my meditation audios alone.

From quick **"Refresher"** sessions for the person who has noticed their growth and achievements slowing down or stagnating, or their enthusiasm waning, lately…

…to my most popular **"Breaking Free!"** program for ANYONE who feels "stuck" or "lost" – held back from a life of freedom and expression by fear, self-doubt, or a set of beliefs that have ball-and-chained them to a hurtful past or some painful present situation…

There's a program that's perfect for your situation!

Perhaps you just need more laser-focused help getting through one particularly difficult transition or challenge. If so, then you'll appreciate my 1-on-1 **"Healing & Growth"** program!

And for the person who would like to experience a **"Total Transformation"** … my 6-month mentoring program goes into incredible depth on the many principles and techniques involved in a total (or at least major) makeover of your current condition – whether you sense a lack in mind, body, spirit, health, relations, finances, or …?

And if you can't decide on the best option for you, then let's schedule a FREE 15-minute consultation call to be sure you're making the BEST choice.

So visit my site today – right now, even, before you put this book down (we both know how easy it is to be distracted by our surroundings). Grab your free gifts, and subscribe to receive updates and messages of support. There's a box right on the Home page to enter your email address into:

www.alenachapmanlife.com

See you online!

Love and Light always –

ABOUT THE AUTHOR

Alena Chapman is a bestselling author, speaker and mentor. She offers on-line courses, as well. Alena's purpose is to share the amazing tools she gained in leaving her own prison behind and opening herself to the wonderful life waiting for her. She helps people leave or change their prisons and achieve their true desires and create happy and fulfilling lives. Be sure to check out Alena's website at http://alen- achapman.com to read her blog, register for Awaken to Freedom Daily Inspirations or the eight week on-line course, "Discovering You." Her book, *You Can't Escape a Prison if You Don't Know You're in One: What is Blocking Your Freedom?* has been endorsed by many people including inspirational master teacher Bob Proctor, national bestselling authors, Peggy McColl and Jennifer Colford.

QUOTE & POEM INDEX

Morgan James
Speakers Group

We connect Morgan James published authors with live and online events and audiences whom will benefit from their expertise.

Printed in the USA
CPSIA information can be obtained
at www.ICGtesting.com
JSHW022329140824
68134JS00019B/1372